# TRIBAL STRENGTHS
## AND
# NATIVE EDUCATION

# Tribal Strengths
## AND
# Native Education

## VOICES FROM THE
## RESERVATION CLASSROOM

## Terry Huffman

University of Massachusetts Press
*Amherst and Boston*

Copyright © 2018 by University of Massachusetts Press
All rights reserved
Printed in the United States of America

ISBN 978-1-62534-303-1 (paper); 302-4 (hardcover)

Set in Adobe Caslon Pro
Printed and bound by The Maple-Vail Book Manufacturing Group

Library of Congress Cataloging-in-Publication Data
Names: Huffman, Terry E., 1958– author.
Title: Tribal strengths and Native education : voices from the reservation
classroom / Terry Huffman.
Description: Amherst : University of Massachusetts Press, [2018] | Includes
bibliographical references and index.
Identifiers: LCCN 2017017172| ISBN 9781625343031 (pbk.) | ISBN 9781625343024
(hardcover)
Subjects: LCSH: Indians of North America—Education. | Indian
teachers—United States. | Indian students—United States. | Indian
reservations—United States.
Classification: LCC E97 .H796 2017 | DDC 371.829/97073—dc23
LC record available at https://lccn.loc.gov/2017017117

British Library Cataloguing-in-Publication Data
A catalog record for this book is available from the British Library.

*Of all the teachings we receive*
*this one is the most important:*
*Nothing belongs to you*
*of what there is,*
*of what you take,*
*you must share.*

*Touch a child—they are my people.*

—CHIEF DAN GEORGE,
*My Heart Soars*

# Contents

# Preface

It seems logical enough that the most appropriate place for scholars and practitioners from around the world to gather and discuss Indigenous education should be . . . Dublin, Ireland. Okay, perhaps not so logical of a location, but there we were in Ireland talking about faraway classrooms in faraway places. The truth is that the gathering occurred at an international conference on education that happened to be held in Dublin. A number of us who were attending also participated in a panel discussion on the opportunities and challenges facing Indigenous education, so perhaps it was not as odd as it first sounds.

Panelists included scholars from Australia, Canada, Kenya, Nigeria, South Africa, and the United States. The discussion that ensued centered on the numerous challenges facing Indigenous peoples, challenges that sound all too familiar to North American tribal nations: the loss of traditional tribal land, threats to cultural integrity (including blatant policies aimed to eradicate the unique culture of Indigenous peoples—most specifically their language), struggles over how to maintain cultural distinctiveness within a dominant society, persistent gaps in academic success for Indigenous students. These are all vexing challenges to be sure, but the discussion also included a robust exchange on the opportunities open to schools and educators serving Indigenous peoples. Here the far-ranging conversation included candid dialogue on culturally sensitive and appropriate pedagogy and curriculum for Indigenous students, culture and language preservation efforts, strategies to enhance academic achievement rates for Indigenous students, and powerful considerations on how schools might be used in reconciliation efforts for nations devastated by tragic racial/ethnic strife.

"Tribal strengths" constitutes the foundational idea of this book. It is an abstract concept but an important one. Tribal strengths includes the general tribal legacy owned by a Native nation that provides its individual members with a specific tribal identity founded on a sense of personal self-concept, social location in relation to others, salient values, and unique worldview. Thus, tribal strengths has two dimensions, the tribal legacy possessed by the nation and the tribal identity expressed by the individual.

In this book I argue that this fundamental concept can be thought of as a keystone. In the construction of an arch, the keystone is the large wedge-shaped stone at the top that locks the other stones in place. In essence, the keystone provides the strength the other stones require for support. Thus, ultimately, tribal strengths involves a symbiotic relationship between tribal identity of the individual person and the tribal legacy of the individual nation. I attempt to convey in this book that tribal strengths empowers both the tribal nation as a whole and people as individuals. But I also try to communicate that reservation schools and Native educators, in particular, are uniquely poised to make significant and enduring contributions to the tribal strengths of their people.

As I reflect on the give-and-take discussions on the issues considered that day in Ireland, it occurs to me they directly connect to the basic premise of this book. On the one hand, the panel engaged in deep conversations on ways in which schools as an institution can provide social good by helping restore cultural loss and preserve cultural heritage. On the other hand, schools can and should positively affect individual students in powerful and enduring ways. As applied to reservation schools and the tribal strengths of Native nations, the lessons are clear. Schools and educators can and should contribute to both the tribal legacy of the nation and the tribal identity of individuals. By helping to preserve tribal cultural traditions and language, reservation schools can play a key role in the continuing vitality of a nation's tribal legacy. What is more, through deliberate and concerted effort, reservation schools can positively affect the tribal identity of Native students.

But that panel discussion in Ireland occurred four years after the beginning of the work that ultimately resulted in this book. In 2010, I began a research project with twenty-one American Indian educators from five reservations in Montana and South Dakota. That research effort focused on a variety of issues, including the roles the educators articulated they play in reservation schools and communities, the rewards and challenges they regard as most prevailing, their experiences in teaching in reservation schools during the era of No Child Left Behind, and their thoughts on the tribal identity issues important to their students and for themselves. That research is reported in a book titled *American Indian Educators in Reservation Schools* published in 2013 by the University of Nevada Press.

After the completion of the research, it was clear there was much more to learn about the tribal identity and tribal legacy issues discussed by the participants. I asked six of the original twenty-one educators to continue the conversation and delve more deeply into these issues. This book results from the interviews and classroom visits with those six American Indian educators serving reservation schools in Montana and South Dakota. Technically, the research is a case study of six Native educators; practically, it involved an ongoing conversation on the meaning and importance of tribal strengths as seen from the classroom experience of six veteran American Indian educational professionals.

Labels are complex and tricky things, all the more so when one has many labels from which to select when describing whole collections of people. When it comes to the first people of the Western Hemisphere, the choices are not only long but potentially controversial. "American Indian," "Native American," "First Nations," "Indigenous peoples," and "tribal nations" are among the labels frequently and, dare I say it, correctly employed to denote the original peoples of North America. In this book I use many of these labels interchangeably—most notably "American Indian," "Native," and "Indigenous people." However, I most frequently use the name American Indian. The reason for this choice is simple. Most typically, tribal members of the Northern Plains of the United States refer to themselves as American Indian. It seems appropriate that I should do so as well. Yet, I do so with the humble understanding that labels are complex and tricky things because they directly connect to a peoples' sovereign right to their cultural identity.

There are many individuals who assisted in the completion of the research reported in this book as well as the writing of the book itself. The support of Scot Headley, dean of the College of Education, George Fox University, and Gary Tiffin, former director of the EdD program,

George Fox University, were especially critical in the completion of the research. My dear friend Ron Ferguson, assistant professor of sociology at Luther College, has offered so much input and critical analysis about my work that I cannot begin to say enough thanks. Nadine Kincaid's generous offer of her central Oregon getaway cabin for me to do some of the writing for the manuscript was a welcome blessing. Of course, it is a great joy to work with Matt Becker, executive editor at the University of Massachusetts Press. Matt is a tremendous professional who really knows his business. I always learn a great deal from him.

Finally, my greatest appreciation and respect go to the six American Indian educators who graciously and patiently sat with me through hours of conversations, opened their classes to me for visits, and showed me around their schools and reservations. Their devotion, professionalism, humility, and humanity I can only hope to somehow convey.

# TRIBAL STRENGTHS
## AND
# NATIVE EDUCATION

# Introduction

American Indians have something different that was bestowed upon them by the grace of God, such as our songs, tribal dances, arts and crafts, our religion, games and stories. Some of these are fast disappearing and my question is: Are we going to continue to lose these precious gifts through this process of education or becoming white men? Or should we continue to identify ourselves as Indians, which to me is no disgrace.

—CLARENCE WESLEY, Chairman, San Carlos Apache Tribe, 1961

I stood in the prairie wind leaning on my car with my head propped up by my right hand. Less than an hour before, I had been informed that the elementary school I was looking for was located down a lonely dirt road leading to a far corner of this particular South Dakota reservation. As I stood there, my worst fear in locating the school had been realized. The road forked in two directions. It is not uncommon for GPS to be next to useless on some western reservations, often indicating roads that do not exist (mine was useless) and without a sign to indicate which way to go (there wasn't a sign); I had to make a choice.[1] So using an old "Indian trick" I had learned years ago, I carefully surveyed the landscape, measured the direction of the wind by dropping a handful of dust, listened to what the birds were trying to tell me . . . and then looked for the school bus tracks in the dirt.

That was the fall of 2010. Since then I have been back to that particular school close to a dozen times, learning more with each visit and becoming a familiar figure to those who work and learn there. I have become close to many of the staff and students. During one visit, I was honored with a brief ceremony that is likely the most important affirmation of my professional and personal life. I have learned a great deal from this particular school as well as other schools like it.

This book is about the voices of educators. It contains the hard-earned reflections of six veteran American Indian educators who faithfully serve in schools located on three different reservations of the Northern Plains. Based on the insights provided by personal interviews, conversations really, I try to articulate how these educators describe the strengths that spring from their tribal heritage and personal ethnicity. I seek to outline their thoughts on the tribal identity issues facing their students and how this identity may be important in academic and life success. I also examine their reflections on the importance of anchoring the formal education of Native children in tribal values and worldview. The refrain of cultural survival derived from tribal strengths serves as the prevailing theme of this book.

The individuals whose voices are heard in the ensuing pages are a unique group. They represent a small number of educators who happen to be Native and serve Native students, schools, and communities. Indeed, because there are so few American Indian educators in reservation schools, their perspectives on tribal strengths and the education of Native children are all the more important. All six individuals I interviewed serve in schools on the reservation where they each have deep personal roots and their tribal memberships. Teaching is more than a career choice; it is an investment in their communities and the future of their tribes. For them, teaching reservation children is very personal, and much is at stake. Thus, at its core, this book is about tribal strengths and American Indian education as seen through the experienced lenses of six veteran Native educators. These individuals understand, both personally and professionally, the importance of tribal strengths as a crucial component in the education of American Indian youth.

A reservation is as much a place of the soul as it is a place on the map. If one is really attentive, you can almost feel the change that occurs upon entering a reservation. I believe such a change involves time and place; the timelessness of cultural heritage and the location of personal belonging. Perhaps one of the most misunderstood aspects of modern-day American Indian reservations is that they are the safe harbors of cultural continuity and survival (DeMillie, 2009). Fixated on the perplexing social problems as we tend to be, it is easy to overlook the fact that many reservations are also places of deep spiritual and cultural roots for Native peoples.[2]

The school I searched for on that day in 2010 plays an important but little recognized role in the cultural continuity and continuance for its reservation and, indeed, for all Lakota people. Virtually all its teachers are Native individuals (a rarity in reservation schools), and a surprising number speak Lakota. Many routinely integrate Lakota values, worldview, and cosmology in their instruction. Perhaps most important, they work hard to foster a positive identity as a Lakota person in the hearts and minds of their young students. Given the history of American Indian education, the way this school operates represents nothing less than an extraordinary and radical transformation in educational philosophy, goals and practice. Indeed, without an understanding of the history of American Indian education, one might never appreciate just how remarkable of a sea change this school and other reservation schools like it are in the educational policy and practice toward Native children. As revealed in the elegant plea offered over a half century ago by San Carlos Apache chairman Clarence Wesley quoted at the opening of this introduction, the tension between cultural survival and educational assimilationist pressures resulted in devastating dilemmas for generations of Native peoples. It is impossible not to be moved by his dignified question—in reality a defiant statement, "Or should we continue to identify ourselves as Indians, which to me is no disgrace."

## Successful Failure:
## A Recent History of American Indian Education

One of the saddest and most unfortunate facts regarding American education is that for decades schools were used in the pursuit of destroying the tribal cultures of Native peoples (Reyhner & Eder, 2004). It was a simple idea with its own logic. American Indian cultures needed to be replaced as quickly and thoroughly as possible with the supposed superior culture of white civilization. As the reasoning of the time went, what institution could possibly be better suited to facilitate the cultural transformation of the Indigenous population than formal education? Moreover, what could be a more efficient system to accomplish cultural assimilation than boarding schools? In this arrangement Native children could be separated from their parents, family, and community and brought under the inclusive sway of non-Indian influence.

For good reasons, boarding schools became the most notorious implements of the assimilationist mission central to the formal education of American Indian children. Nowhere is this mission more blatantly and obnoxiously found than in the informal motto associated with the Carlisle Indian School: "Kill the Indian to save the man" (Carney, 1999). Founded in 1879 by career army officer Richard Pratt, the Carlisle Indian School of Pennsylvania, and the many other boarding schools modeled after it, held as a virtually singular mission the cultural assimilation of Native children.[3] In an address to the Conference of Charities and Corrections held in Denver in 1892, Pratt famously outlined his philosophy on the education of Native youth. He began his remarks by declaring, "A great general has said that the only good Indian is a dead one, and that high sanction of his destruction has been an enormous factor in promoting Indian massacres. In a sense, I agree with the sentiment, but only in this: that all the Indian there is in the race should be dead. Kill the Indian in him, and save the man"[4] (Pratt, 1973, p. 260).

With the widespread acceptance of this culturally imperialistic educational philosophy, the chase was on in a way never before seen in the history of American Indian education. Late nineteenth-century educational reformers, who sincerely believed they were doing social good through saving Native students' humanity by destroying their very ethnicity, led the pursuit. As David Wallace Adams (1995), in his devastating book *Education for Extinction,* explains:

> In retrospect it is not surprising that reformers should look to schools as central to the Indian problem. As an instrument of fostering social cohesion and republicanism, no institution had been more important in the spread of the American system. In the case of Indians the challenge facing educators was particularly difficult: the eradication of all traces of tribal identity and culture, replacing them with the commonplace knowledge and values of white civilization . . . Boarding schools, especially the off-reservation variety, seemed ideally suited for this purpose. As the theory went, Indian children, once removed from the savage surroundings of the Indian camp and placed in the purified environment of an all-encompassing institution, would slowly learn to look, act, and eventually think like their white counterparts . . . When it was all

over, the one-time youthful specimens of savagism would be thoroughly Christianized, individualized, and republicanized, fit candidates for American citizenship and ideal agents for uplifting an older generation still stranded in the backwaters of barbarism—"a little child shall lead them." (p. 335)

It was not a gentle form of assimilation offered by boarding schools either; the process was compulsory and very often physically and emotionally brutal (Szasz, 1999). What is more, the negative effects of boarding schools did not end with the early 1900s. It would be a serious mistake to believe the ill consequences of boarding schools are simply the residue of a bygone era. Largely as a result of the forcefulness, ruthlessness, and arrogance of many boarding schools, they have left an indelible legacy. Much of the apathy toward education found in many reservations today can be directly traced back to the abuses suffered during the boarding school experiences for generations of American Indians (Huffman, 2013; Peshkin, 1997).

It would also be erroneous to think that the impact of some boarding schools was only cultural assimilation. More than cultural imperialism occurred in many of these schools; some institutions engaged in the systematic, concerted effort to destroy the human spirit itself (Adams, 1995; Archuleta, Child, & Lomawaima, 2000; Child, 1998; Colmant et al., 2004; Lomawaima, 1994). But the combination of forced cultural domination and the breaking of an individual's spirit has not occurred without a backlash of determined reaction. In recent years thousands of American Indians have been striking back against past indignities and abuses incurred while enrolled in boarding schools. A number of important lawsuits have been filed against the federal government and private institutions, most notably the Catholic Church, for alleged abuses of Native children. One of the largest was a $25 billion class action suit filed in the US Court of Federal Claims in Washington, DC, on behalf of scores of American Indians for physical, sexual, and psychological abuse suffered while attending South Dakota Catholic boarding schools (Colmant et al., 2004; Waxman, 2003). Representative of so many of the other legal actions (only on a grander scale), this incredibly complex lawsuit against the federal government (which paid the Church to house, feed, and educate Native students) claimed that many of these children were subjected to outrageous abuses.[5] As *Washington Post* journalist

Sharon Waxman (2003) reported, "Allegations of priestly sexual abuse in parishes have rocked the Catholic Church over the past year. But what the former students say occurred at reservation schools into the 1970s was more systematic: They say that physical abuse was a routine part of school discipline; that sexual abuse was commonplace; and that both forms of abuse were committed against children in the round-the-clock, unsupervised care of school staff members" (p. A01).

Yet despite the concerted assault on Native cultures, extraordinary resistance and cultural perseverance are also important chapters in the story of American Indian education. While many tribal cultures are certainly seriously endangered, a significant number have endured. This cultural doggedness was only possible because of the brave individual and collective efforts of tribal peoples. Even in the face of the extreme attempts at the most aggressive boarding schools, resistance and determination undermined the assimilationist mission (Lomawaima & McCarty, 2006). Some scholars contend that the very attempts at cultural assimilation actually resulted in the strengthening of tribal identity for many Native students. In an ironic twist, the assimilationist efforts of educators backfired and led to tribal resurgence in ways not possible without such institutions as boarding schools. Trafzer, Keller, and Sisquoc (2006) make the interesting argument that:

> among North American Indians, the boarding school system was a successful failure. The practice of removing Native American children from their homes, families, and communities and forcing them into an educational system designed to assimilate them into American and Canadian societies both succeeded and failed. The governments succeeded in providing some measure of academic, domestic, agricultural, and vocational education to First Nations children, but they failed to assimilate completely Indian children or entirely destroy the essence of their being Native peoples. Ironically, the American boarding school and Canadian residential school experience for many Native American children provided new skills in language, literature, mathematics, and history that strengthened their identities as Native Americans. Many children attending boarding schools returned home or moved to urban areas where they embraced their American Indian heritage in a heightened manner, communicating their strength in being the First Americans in ways that preserved Indian identity. Thus the very system that non-Indians had established to "Kill the Indian in him and save the man" provided Indian students with the experience and expertise to

"turn the power." Students used the potentially negative experience to produce a positive result—the preservation of Indian identity, cultures, communities, languages, and peoples. (p. 1)

We tend to think of boarding schools as associated with the late nineteenth and early twentieth centuries. However, boarding schools for Native students actually witnessed the height of their enrollments during the 1950s and 1960s[6] (Wilkinson, 2005). To understand why this was the case, one needs to consider the nature of federal policies toward Native nations following World War II.

Upon the conclusion of the Second World War, the federal government could once again turn its attention more fully to domestic concerns. American Indian policy soon came to the attention of first the Truman and then the Eisenhower administration (Ulrich, 2010). Both administrations regarded the integration of Native peoples into the mainstream society as the solution to American Indian social problems. It was the old notion of assimilation put into effect with a full head of steam. If Native peoples could not be gently guided into assimilation, then they would have to be coerced and pushed into situations where they would have no other alternative. To fulfill this social/cultural goal, the federal government introduced a new policy—termination. Along with this new policy direction came a companion program called "relocation." It is important to understand that termination was the parent policy, whereas relocation (at least originally) was merely a program established to help accomplish the larger goals of the termination policy. With time, however, as termination fell into disfavor, relocation evolved into its own independent policy, essentially outliving its parent policy.

While the events leading up to the establishment of the policy of termination and the legal entanglements surrounding it were enormously complex, its goal was surprisingly simple (Fixico, 1986). Dillon S. Myer, the Truman appointee as commissioner of Indian Affairs (one of the major architects of termination), stated the goal of the policy in unequivocal terms in a letter addressed to the secretary of the interior in 1953: "Let us put the Indian Bureau out of business" (Myer, 1970).[7] A grandfatherly looking man from Ohio, Myer has become a favorite target of historians and other pundits of federal American Indian policy, some of whom have gone to great lengths to demonize him as a particularly loathsome character in the history of American racism (see, for instance,

Drinnon, 1987). It is certainly easy to understand the reasons why. It was the same Dillon S. Myer who was in charge of the infamous relocation centers for Japanese Americans during World War II. In fairness, Myer actually said the Bureau of Indian Affairs should get out of business as quickly as possible but that the job must be "done with honor." Be that as it may, what began with Myer's appointment and continued after his departure can hardly be described as honorable. The policy of termination sought to end Bureau of Indian Affairs services and treaty responsibilities to tribes. In simple terms, termination meant that the federal government ceased to recognize the sovereignty of tribes and ended the trust relationship over their reservation lands. Thus, targeted nations lost their status as acknowledged tribes as well as their land as recognized reservations. More bluntly, termination meant that the federal government ceased to recognize terminated tribes as legitimate Native nations. At the federal level, terminated tribes were stripped of their very identity. For a proud, ancient people, this was a cruel indignity. Yet, for many of the terminated tribes, the worst was yet to come.

In 1953 Senator Arthur Watkins of Utah (another major architect of termination) introduced a series of legislative acts designed to end federal responsibilities to American Indian tribes and terminate the special legal status of reservation lands.[8] These various legislative pieces were eventually combined into House Concurrent Resolution 108, more commonly known as the Termination Act of 1953, which authorized the transfer of federal services to the appropriate state agencies (or ended those services outright). It also set in motion the termination of selected reservations as federally recognized land areas.

As the policy of termination emerged, an obvious question also arose, that is, what to do with the people who lost their reservations and health and educational services. To this difficulty Commissioner Myer had an answer. American Indians of terminated tribes must be "relocated" to urban areas so they could better assimilate into mainstream society and, supposedly, become more self-sufficient. Given the notoriety of Dillon S. Myer as the director of the relocation centers for Japanese Americans during the war, one can only speculate on the chilling effect the first announcement of a relocation program for American Indians must have had on reservations. Nevertheless, to help accomplish the objectives of the Termination Act of 1953, Congress passed the Indian Relocation Act of 1956, which authorized the federal government to pay the moving costs and subsidize vocational training for American Indians willing to move to targeted urban centers. Thus, relocation became an essential program to help accomplish the goals of the policy of termination. Ultimately, relocation centers were established in Chicago, Cleveland, Dallas, Denver, Los Angeles, Oakland, San Francisco, and San Jose. Although estimates vary, approximately 100,000 people were officially "relocated" by the time Congress and the Bureau of Indian Affairs ended the program (Fixico, 2000).

For a time, relocation enjoyed wide political support. Not only was it favored among conservative politicians, but many significant liberal political figures of the day also embraced relocation and regarded it as a brilliant answer to the elusive question of the place of Native peoples in modern American society. Such figures as Lyndon Johnson, Hubert Humphrey, Robert Kennedy, and Ted Kennedy all endorsed relocation and predicted the success of the program.

Curiously, while termination was clearly one of the most aggressive assimilationist policies in federal history, relocation, so warmly endorsed by liberal politicians, was at its core essentially an assimilationist directive. Ultimately, relocation too failed to realize any real success as American Indian policy. Although large numbers of Native people were relocated to cities, many, if not most, found life in urban America extremely difficult. Many discovered they had simply traded rural poverty for urban poverty. By the Bureau of Indian Affairs' own admission, nearly three of every ten relocated American Indians returned home during their first year in a city. Some critics have suggested the eventual proportion of people returning to their former reservations might have been as high as 75 percent (Fixico, 2000). Relocation as the answer to American Indian problems was abandoned by 1972.

Termination is widely recognized as one of the worst failures and most morally bankrupt policies since the pursuit of armed conflict as an American Indian policy (Deloria, 1969; Fixico, 1986). The termination policy also had a disastrous effect on Native peoples. Tribes were virtually universally unprepared for the radical, abrupt termination of their sovereignty status and the associated treaty and trust obligations. During the brief period of this policy, Congress terminated 109 tribal nations involving 13,263 people and the loss of over 1.3 million acres of land (Fixico, 1986; Ulrich, 2010). Although this represented only about 3 percent of all tribally enrolled Native people, termination caused tremendous anxiety and a hostility among tribal nations that endures to this day (Ulrich, 2010). As hard as it is to believe, even worse than the loss of reservation land were the consequences associated with the loss of basic human services, especially health services. The policy of termination was so detrimental that it lived a relatively short life—only eleven years. The last termination of a tribe occurred in 1964. In 1971 the United States Senate took an unprecedented step by disavowing the entire termination policy and apologizing for this legislative action.

Both termination and relocation had tremendous impacts on American Indian education. With the introduction of termination and relocation, many officials, especially those within the Bureau of Indian Affairs, encouraged schools serving Native children to refocus their curriculum on education for urban life (Cornell & Kalt, 2010; Fixico, 2000). However, even more significant than altering curriculum was the loss of such services as schools serving Native students. With the termination of services, many former reservations found their schools closed. Thus enrollments in boarding schools increased during the 1950s and 1960s simply because children of terminated tribes frequently did not have any local school to attend.

The 1960s witnessed the civil rights movement, the antiwar movement, and a general increased awareness over social concerns. As America struggled with the issue of civil rights, expanded notions of racial fairness and social justice emerged. The drive for greater American Indian autonomy over their affairs reached a turning point during this time, helped in large part by three major events, all spearheaded by the newly formed, intentionally provocative, and immediately controversial American Indian Movement (AIM). In 1969 American Indian activists occupied Alcatraz Island (earlier abandoned as a federal penitentiary), in 1972 they staged the Trail of Broken Treaties to protest social and economic conditions of American Indians (the event ended with the spontaneous takeover of the Bureau of Indian Affairs offices in Washington, DC), and in 1973 AIM became involved in the highly publicized and dramatic siege of Wounded Knee on the Pine Ridge reservation in South Dakota.[9]

Central to these events was disgust over the misguided and heavy-handed federal policies of the past. In particular, American Indian

activists remonstrated that the highly paternalistic policies of termination and relocation were merely methods of control and demanded
greater autonomy over tribal affairs. They called for nothing less than
tribal sovereignty (Cornell & Kalt, 2010). These activities generated a
great deal of hostility from federal and state authorities. In fact, anything
and anyone associated with AIM invited instant suspicion and reaction,
especially from federal officials (Smith & Warrior, 1996). Nevertheless,
ultimately, the protests of American Indian activists did not fall on deaf
ears. Both the interested public and the government were ready for significant changes in federal American Indian policy.

In July 1970, President Richard Nixon outlined the need for a new
federal policy in a Special Message on Indian Affairs delivered to Congress. As Cornell and Kalt (2010) explain, "The statement underscored
the federal government's trust responsibility, while altering the focus of
US policy in meeting that responsibility. President Nixon's vision for a
new direction in policy included a shift in responsibility for the control
over public programs to tribal governments under the precept that local
self-rule (in this case by self-governing Indian tribes) would be better
able to promote the federal government's trust responsibility for the
socioeconomic well-being of tribal citizens" (p. 18). Thus, Nixon's message signaled the end of policies of the past. The new policy became that
of self-determination.

At its most basic, the policy of self-determination sought to achieve
greater self-government for American Indian tribes. Tribes would be
treated essentially as states within states (Cornell & Kalt, 2010). Under
self-determination, a tribe would still be subject to federal law but, like
each state, would have its own constitution and administer its own
internal civil systems. Although President Nixon first signaled the shift
in federal Indian policy toward self-determination in 1970, it took four
years to craft the proper legislation to officially establish the policy. On
January 4, 1975, President Gerald Ford signed into law the Indian Self-
Determination and Education Assistance Act. The enactment of this
legislation has proven to be a watershed event in the history of not only
American Indian education but also in federal American Indian policy
itself.

One of the manifest functions of the Indian Self-Determination
and Education Assistance Act was that tribes would at last gain control

over the formal education of their children. Under the policy of self-determination, schools are more sensitive to the cultural needs of Native children as never before. Nevertheless, significant challenges remain even in this new era of self-determination. Some of these challenges arise from attempting to meet top-down educational policy mandates such as those found in No Child Left Behind and its initiative descendants (i.e., Race to the Top and Common Core) while also providing sufficient instructional vigor and time toward tribally focused education needs such as tribal languages, history, and culture (McCarty, 2008; Winstead, Lawrence, Brantmeier, & Frey, 2008). Other challenges result simply from the patchwork of schools that serve American Indian families from reservation communities. Although not all these options may be available to reservation families, four different kinds of schools commonly serve reservations: tribal schools; state-administered schools; private boarding schools; and schools administered by the Bureau of Indian Education (BIE).

Some reservations administer their own tribal schools. Typical is the Crow Creek Tribal School District located on the Crow Creek reservation of South Dakota. In this case the Crow Creek Lakota administer their own school system modeled after state-run schools. However, the tribe has complete control and responsibility for the schools. Many reservations have entered into special agreements with the state for educational services. These agreements, known as a memo of understanding (MOU), designate how long the arrangement will last and for what obligations each party will be responsible. An example is the Warm Springs reservation in Oregon, which has a MOU with the Jefferson County School District. Private boarding schools, almost all of which are affiliated with a religious group, still play a significant role in American Indian education. Some of these schools are found on the reservation, such as St. Francis Indian School, on the Rosebud reservation in South Dakota; others are located off a reservation, such as St. Joseph's Indian School in Chamberlain, South Dakota. The federal government still plays a role (albeit minor compared with decades past) in American Indian education. Today the Bureau of Indian Education is the federal arm which oversees American Indian education. The BIE operates a number of important boarding schools. Like private boarding schools, some of the BIE schools are located on reservations or other tribally designated areas. An example is the Flandreau Indian School located in Flandreau,

South Dakota. Some BIE schools are located away from reservations, as is the Chemawa Indian School in Salem, Oregon.

## The Shifting Winds of American Indian Education Scholarship

When one ponders the last half of the twentieth century, federal American Indian policy transitioned much more quickly than did the philosophy guiding the education of Native students. Consider that during the 1950s the federal policy toward Native tribes involved termination and relocation, explicit attempts at cultural assimilation, yet by the 1970s, federal policy had shifted to self-determination. In only about twenty years, federal policy moved from the termination of tribal status for Native nations to providing greater autonomy and self-government for tribes. One has to admit this change was a radical shift in policy direction in a relatively short span of time. Yet, the prevailing educational theory surrounding the means to achieve greater academic success for Native students did not change very much—not at first, at least.

Even as assimilationist and paternalistic policies of the federal government came under critical evaluation and eventual reform, a significant number of scholars and practitioners involved in American Indian education either explicitly or implicitly continued to subscribe to what is generally known as the "cultural deficit theory of education" (Huffman, 2010). Cultural deficit theory is not a unified theory as such; in actuality it is a collection of loosely held assumptions tied together by a basic premise. Further, scholars refer to cultural deficit theory by different labels (e.g., cultural deprivation theory). It is also related to what is often called "deficit thinking" or "deficit theory" in education. The common denominator for all these strands is the notion that families deeply entrenched in impoverished situations hold specific values and display normative behaviors that are functional for survival in the desperate conditions of poverty but also place their children at a gross disadvantage in schools which tend to operate according to middle-class expectations (Valencia, 2010).

The fundamental assumptions central to cultural deficit theory first took formal shape with the work of anthropologist Oscar Lewis with the introduction of his "culture of poverty" thesis in the late 1950s (Lewis,

1959). Cultural deficit theory has experienced a more recent revival in the highly popular but equally controversial work of Ruby Payne (2005) in which she argues for a framework for understanding how hidden rules work to discourage poor people from overcoming their circumstances. The basic premise of both Lewis and Payne is essentially the same: the poor are culturally different from other Americans, and this dissimilarity presents a serious barrier toward greater educational success and the potential means to escape impoverished conditions.

The culture of poverty thesis gained a great deal of popularity in the 1960s (not coincidentally during the time of the War on Poverty), and an army of social scientists began to lay down the basic theoretical themes that would be given new life in the first decade of the twenty-first century. Namely, it was widely accepted that the lack of educational achievement common among the poor (and especially poor minorities) was because they lacked an intellectually stimulating home environment (Bloom, Davis, & Hess, 1965). Many poor families hampered by the crushing weight of impoverished conditions, survival mentalities, and values developed around immediate needs rather than long-term goals were simply socially disadvantaged and failed to value education or provide the home learning environment necessary for academic success[10] (Biber, 1967; Chafel, 1997; Crow, Murray, & Smythe, 1966).

Cultural deficit theory appeals to some scholars and practitioners for a number of reasons. Intuitively, it does resonate that poverty is a major impediment to educational achievement (Jensen, 2009). Additionally, poverty, along with its frequent by-products (e.g., poor health, substandard living conditions, high rates of neighborhood crime, etc.), is frustratingly difficult to alleviate and therefore frequently persists generation to generation, creating what may appear to be something akin to a unique culture (Neuman, 2008). It should also be pointed out that according to cultural deficit theory, the source of academic failure for poor students is located outside the school, not within it, perhaps not an insignificant reason for its popularity among some educators[11] (Erickson, 1987; Gans, 1995; Gorski, 2008).

Not surprising, however, cultural deficit theory has met with widespread criticism. In particular, critics find objectionable the ethnocentric logic contained within the perspective (Banfield, 1977; Erickson, 1987; Gorski, 2008; Ryan, 1976). Some scholars have even attacked cultural deficit thinking as thinly veiled racism. Tara Yosso (2005), for instance, challenges, "One of the most prevalent forms of contemporary racism in US schools is deficit thinking" (p. 75). She continues by arguing, "Deficit thinking takes the position that minority students and families are at fault for poor academic performance because: (a) students enter school without the normative cultural knowledge and skills; and (b) parents neither value nor support their child's education. These racialized assumptions about Communities of Color most often lead schools to default to the banking method of education critiqued by Paulo Freire (1973). As a result, schooling efforts usually aim to fill up supposedly passive students with forms of cultural knowledge deemed valuable by dominant society" (p. 75).

Despite prevailing criticisms, cultural deficit theory enjoyed an influential run through the 1960s to the late 1980s, fell out of favor for about ten years, and experienced a sudden resurgence in the late 1990s largely owing to the popularity of Ruby Payne's work. As used today, scholars (who generally do not refer themselves as cultural deficit theorists) tend to underscore the responsibility of educators to inform themselves on the negative effects of poverty while also recognizing the inherent ability for all children to learn under the proper guidance of competent teachers. These scholars tend to emphasize the accountability of educators in ways not stressed in years past (Jensen, 2009). Even so, many critics are highly skeptical of what they consider to be little more than stereotypical characterizations of the poor advanced by Payne and her adherents (Bomer, Dworin, May, & Semingson, 2008; Gorski, 2008; Ng & Rury, 2005; Osei-Kofi, 2005).

What is especially noteworthy here is the specific way in which cultural deficit theory has been used to understand the educational experiences of American Indian students. More to the point, in the hands of many scholars of Native education, the cultural deficit perspective gained an added dimension. It was not only the deficiencies associated with poverty that work against some Native students but also their very affiliation with tribal cultural traditions, identity, and sometimes communities that were thought to impede educational success (Miller, 1971; Scott, 1986). In other words, tribal cultures are considered barriers to academic achievement rather than strengths to facilitate educational success (Forbes, 2000; Huffman, 2010).

For the greater part of the twentieth century, a significant number of American Indian education scholars and practitioners widely and uncritically accepted the assumption that cultural assimilation would invite greater academic success for individual Native students and lead to the general betterment of tribal peoples as a whole. It was nothing more than the old notion of assimilation attired in academic robes. This theoretical assumption maintained a strong beachhead in American Indian education scholarship for a very long time and proved to be highly influential in shaping classroom pedagogical practices (Deloria & Wildcat, 2001; Swisher & Tippeconnic, 1999). Indeed, some of the earliest published, peer-reviewed scholarship in the field of American Indian education reflected a cultural deficit perspective with the supplementary (and seemingly obligatory) call for greater cultural assimilation. In 1961, David O. Lloyd, at the time director of guidance and special services for the Mesa, Arizona, public school system, published findings from a study comparing the academic performance and intelligence quotients of American Indian and white students enrolled in Mesa public high schools. Predictably, Native students fared far worse on all measures compared with whites. As a further examination, Lloyd then compared the intelligence quotients of Native students who had spent their entire educational experience in the Mesa public school system (and presumably had greater exposure to the assimilating effects of the system) with Native students who had been enrolled in the public school system for only one or two years (and thus had less exposure to those same presumed assimilation influences). Lloyd reported that "there seems to be evidence that those Indians who have spent their entire educational life in the Mesa Public Schools tend to have a higher mean intelligence quotient for language, non-language and total mental as measured by the California Test of Mental Maturity than those who have been in the system a relatively short time" (p. 12). Regarding the overall nature and implications of his findings, Lloyd concluded by declaring:

> At the present time, the total Indian population in the Mesa Public Schools, as a group, has not attained the same intellectual and academic heights, as measured by standardized tests, as those attained by the non-Indian . . . There appear to be many sociological and psychological factors that may account for the results shown in this article. Chief among

them may be the fact that while the Indian student is in an integrated system during the school day, he spends the major portion of his life in a segregated situation where the socioeconomic standard is much lower and where many of the enriching experiences are lacking . . . The cultural background of the Indian is still quite different than that of the non-Indian population and while strides are being made toward the assimilation of the Indian into the non-Indian culture, there is still much to be accomplished. (pp. 15–16)

In many respects this particular article is unexceptional and is typical for the Indigenous education scholarship of that period. What makes it particularly striking is that Lloyd's article appeared in the inaugural edition of the *Journal of American Indian Education,* a peer-reviewed scholarly organ with the stated mission to advance scholarship and understanding on Native educational issues. For five decades this journal has consistently provided an enormously important service through its publication of high-quality, relevant scholarship. Yet the fact that this article reporting conclusions firmly grounded on an assimilationist version of cultural deficit theory is so prominently found in the first issue of the first volume of this periodical demonstrates just how widely these views were accepted.

The latter part of the twentieth century witnessed a variety of interesting, absurd, engaging, and downright ridiculous attempts to tie American Indian educational achievement to greater cultural assimilation. One of the more provocative accounts held that the reason for the lack of educational success among Lakota young men was that they were essentially "warriors without weapons" (Deloria, 1969, p. 95). Based on extensive ethnographic fieldwork on the Pine Ridge reservation during the 1950s and 1960s, anthropologist Rosalie Wax (1967) was perplexed by the educational difficulties among the reservation's youth, especially teenaged boys. As she contemplated the dynamics involved in the lack of academic success, she eventually concluded that the problem was that the Lakota youth had become "warrior dropouts."

The idea was a simple one. According to Wax, traditional Lakota culture values bravado and acts of audacity among young men. Unfortunately, these same attributes are not only discouraged in formal school settings but also considered highly disruptive and dysfunctional. As a result, young Lakota men are caught in a tension created by the socialization of the cultural community of which they are a part and the expectations of the educational institution that they must attend. Mounting frustration over appropriate outlets for their cultural values and behaviors eventually lead the young men to reject the school and drop out, becoming, in Wax's words, "warrior dropouts."

The warrior dropout thesis generated much interest, but it also drew a great deal of criticism for its oversimplified logic and stereotypical portrayal of Lakota life (as well as a general misunderstanding of Lakota culture).[12] By far the most entertaining criticism came from the late Vine Deloria Jr. (1969), who suggested that perhaps the solution to the educational problems facing students at the Pine Ridge reservation was for the Bureau of Indian Affairs to run a wagon load of treaty annuities through the agency headquarters and allow teenage boys to "attack" it in sham raid, thereby alleviating their displaced warrior frustrations. They could be back in school and ready to learn the next day.

A significant number of scholars held to the notion that tribal culture is an impediment to educational success into the last decades of the twentieth century. Even as late as 1986, in an assessment of the college experience for Native students, Wilbur Scott credited a strong connection to tribal culture as the reason for the lack of educational success: "The findings clearly show that being a 'cultural Indian' reduces the chances of academic success. Independent of all other considerations, including how much measured academic ability the student has, such a student is more likely to fail because he or she is less likely to become integrated into the university community. The findings are important because they identify the process through which attachment to Indian culture affects academic success and because they implicate the role of the university setting in encouraging failure" (pp. 392–93). While Scott proceeds to criticize the university for creating structural systems that allow little room for Native students to embrace and utilize their cultural identity, he still cannot quite resist the call for eventual greater assimilation:

> Historically, the assumed course of change in Indian-white relations has been unidirectional: Indians have been expected to become "white" cheerfully. In the case of education, Indian students have been counseled to become "less Indian" as a conscious strategy for doing better in school. If this is what is meant by success, many Indians would not consider dropping out of school a mark of failure. For many, success in education

means mastering white ways on one's own terms by maintaining some commitment to Indian values and traditions. *The issue is not whether assimilation should take place but rather how much, how fast, and under whose directions.* (p. 393, italics added)

Assimilationist assumptions, even supposed kinder, gentler forms such as those expressed by Scott, survived a long time, and when they eventually died, they died a hard death. In the early years of my own career, my work frequently ran afoul of cultural deficit scholars highly critical of any theoretical perspective that challenged established and accepted assimilationist assumptions. But when the theoretical winds shifted in American Indian education studies, they changed radically and powerfully. And those winds blew completely in the opposite direction. By the 1990s a strong contingent of scholars (perhaps a majority of whom are Native persons) provided new voices to the American Indian education conversation. For the first time in the history of American Indian educational studies, the aging assimilationist perspectives were effectively countered by rigorous empirical evidence along with vigorous arguments refuting long-held assumptions. Today, tribal identity and culture are generally regarded as strengths that facilitate academic success rather than impediments to achievement. Indeed, a growing body of evidence documents the connection between a strong tribal identity and academic accomplishment. From studies with young primary students (Powers, 2005, 2006; Whitbeck, Hoyt, Stubben, & LaFromboise, 2001) to high school students (Cleary & Peacock, 1998; Valdas, 1995; Ward, 2005), to college undergraduate and graduate students (Huffman, 2008; Lindley, 2009; White Shield, 2009), researchers consistently find that a strong affinity with one's tribal heritage is the key to academic success.

If cultural assimilation is the theme for most of the history of American Indian education, determined cultural resilience is the often overlooked consequence of that history. There is a power to tribal strengths that defies attempts at cultural extermination. Roland Tharp (2006) makes such a point when he argues: "Every attempt at behavior influence and change of Native American populations by Euro-American institutions has been impotent. This includes the infamous boarding schools of the earlier 20th century, into which Indian youth were forced. The boarding schools did wreak havoc on Indian native languages, and on the cultural continuity of parenting skills, but their academic successes were slight, and their purpose of destroying Indian identity failed utterly" (p. 7).

The key point made by Tharp is that the attempt to destroy "Indian identity failed utterly." The resolute claim to an America Indian identity, for individuals as well as tribes, is basic to cultural resilience. What is more, as Tharp and so many others point out, forced assimilation tactics failed to produce academic success. Ultimately, assimilationist-based education efforts resulted in greater alienation of Native students, intensified cultural hostilities, facilitated the tragic loss of tribal languages, and left a legacy of resentment among tribes toward education as an institution—but they did not kill the spirit. Likely few understand this better than Native educators who teach in reservation classrooms.

As we stand in the opening decades of the twenty-first century, we have witnessed a virtual complete reversal in federal American Indian policy and educational philosophy from the larger part of the nineteenth and twentieth centuries. The challenge now remains for educators, especially Native educators, to seize the opportunity and realize the potential provided by the full expression of tribal strengths.

# 1

## Voices from the Reservation Classroom

I believe tribal identity is a key for success for our students. You have to start with who you are and have that pride and say because I'm a Native American this is what I want to do for myself and for my people.

—LORI, South Dakota educator

The North Dakota wind blew through the cracks in the crude clapboard walls of the Fort Yates school. The children shivered and lightly tapped their toes to help with the blood circulation. Some of the adults, Natives and a few whites, blew into their hands to keep warm. The tiny stove in the corner of the room fought a valiant yet largely vain battle against the November winter. Despite their discomfort, those present remained silent and respectful as the great man began to speak. It was one of the few times Sitting Bull specifically addressed the formal, Western-styled education of his people. But on this gray morning with snow lightly dusting the prairie, he summed up a new vision for the *wakanyeja*, the sacred beings—the children.[1]

In the clear and confident voice that was his trademark, Sitting Bull intoned, "I have advised my people thus: when you find anything good in the white man's road, pick it up; but when you find something bad, or that turns out bad, drop it, leave it alone."[2] It was a remarkable endorsement. Sitting Bull had spent the greater part of his life actively resisting the institutions and values of white society. Yet, on this bleak November day in 1890 he not only identified but validated a new path for his people (Vestal, 1934).

In just over a month Sitting Bull would be dead, cut down in a hail of vengeful, angry bullets just outside his cabin on the Standing Rock reservation. As those who were killed in the frenzied madness on the morning of December 29, 1890, at Wounded Knee in the newly formed state of South Dakota were refugees from the Standing Rock and Cheyenne River reservations seeking protection from the last great chief Red Cloud, it is likely that some of the Hunkpapa Lakota children who heard Sitting Bull's hopeful words too would lie dead. Their bloodied, mangled bodies, covered by a blizzard, would eventually be unceremoniously buried in a mass grave atop a lonely hill. They rest there to this day.

Wounded Knee has become a powerful symbol in American history. It represents the final military defeat of American Indians in the United States. As a dark cloud hanging over American history, Wounded Knee is also emblematic of the horrific consequences unleased by unfettered racism. In the days following Sitting Bull's murder (and only a week before the massacre at Wounded Knee), the *Aberdeen (SD) Saturday Pioneer* ran an editorial written by its publisher and one of Aberdeen's leading citizens:

> Sitting Bull, the most renowned Sioux of modern history is dead . . . The proud spirit of the original owners of these vast prairies inherited through centuries of fierce and bloody wars for their possession, lingered last in the bosom of Sitting Bull. With his fall the nobility of the Redskin is exterminated, and what few are left are a pack of whining curs who lick the hand that smites them. The Whites, by law of conquer, by justice of civilization, are masters of the American continent, and the best safety of the frontier settlements will be secured by the total annihilation of the few remaining Indians. Why annihilation? Their glory has fled, their spirit broken, their manhood effaced; better that they die than live the miserable wretches that they are. (Di Silvestro, 2005, pp. 84–85)

Five days after the horror at Wounded Knee, the same editorialist offered a stark recommendation: "The *Pioneer* has before declared that our only safety depends upon the total extermination of the Indians. Having wronged them for centuries we had better in order to protect our civilization, follow it up by one more wrong and wipe these untamed and untamable creatures from the face of the earth" (Hastings, 2007, para. 4) Ten years later the editorialist, L. Frank Baum, would write the acclaimed *The Wonderful Wizard of Oz*.

The tragedy at Wounded Knee has taken its heartbreaking place alongside other utterly incomprehensible atrocities over the last century and a half. Sand Creek, Armenia, Auschwitz, My Lai, Tuol Sleng prison, Danfur, Srebrenica: the blood-soaked list seems to have no end. The maelstrom of violence that exploded in South Dakota in late December 1890 and for the first week of January 1891 marked the end of the so-called Indian Wars of the late nineteenth century and ushered in a new chapter in American Indian affairs. A new era, it might be added, that would have its own frequent heartbreaks, misguided intentions, and cruel outbursts. Yet this period would also witness unexpected breakthroughs, hard-won victories, and promising new beginnings. Sitting Bull's vision would not be lost and forgotten within the cold walls of a Fort Yates, North Dakota, schoolhouse. That vision lives on and has taken on a vitality that might have surprised even him. His words would prove to be the compelling challenge for a new generation of American Indians. "But we will retain our beauty and still be Indians" is not just rhetoric to this new generation; it is also the only realistic means for survival.

To the rational mind it seems virtually impossible that Native tribal cultures have survived at all. Centuries of unrelenting assault on tribal peoples and their cultures resulted in unfathomable physical and cultural loss. Demographer Russell Thornton (1987) estimates that from the time Europeans landed in the Bahamas in 1492 until the Wounded Knee tragedy in 1890, approximately 50 million Native people were killed by war, starvation, and European-borne diseases. The devastation to the lands they originally occupied is so vast that they can be seen with the naked eye from the International Space Station. What is more, Native peoples suffered some of their worst losses in the United States. Thornton estimates that by 1890 US tribes had the lowest survival rate for any Indigenous people in the world. Approximately two-thirds of the original tribes living in what is now the United States completely vanished from the earth. Indeed, by 1890 only about 250,000 American Indians survived. Then, and today, American Indians constitute less than 2 percent of the US population (US Census Bureau, 2010).

Invaluable, irreplaceable cultural wisdom has been lost, tribal languages forever silenced. Today one of the most urgent concerns for tribal
peoples centers on the impending loss of ancient languages and the
irreparable cultural damage occasioned by that loss. As one American
Indian educator lamented, "I really fear for my people here because our
language teacher in the school has retired and the people that speak the
language, they're getting older, and they're dying. So it's like, okay, who's
going to carry that on when they're gone? It's scary because our whole
culture is in that language" (Huffman, 2013, p. 138).

But Sitting Bull's vision remains, and despite all the odds, hope per-
vades on American Indian reservations. While conducting a workshop
at the University of South Dakota, I discussed my recent research with
American Indian educators serving reservation schools (Huffman, 2013).
Part of the presentation included a discussion on the serious challenges
facing reservation educators. Pervasive poverty, student suicide, deaths
due to substance abuse, child neglect and abuse among other assorted
social problems complicate and frequently frustrate the efforts of these
professionals. During the question-and-answer session, a faculty member related she had taught for many years in one of the nation's largest
inner cities. The challenges I mentioned were the same as those facing the
educators in those schools. So, she asked, what is the difference between
the experiences of these two sets of professional educators? My answer
was that the difference is simple yet significant.

In so many of our inner-city communities, there appears very little
hope for change and for the future. It is a sadness of spirit borne from
years of frustration and injustice. In late 2014, when Ferguson, Missouri,
exploded in anger over a grand jury's decision not to indict Darren Wilson, a white police officer, in the shooting death of unarmed Michael
Brown, an eighteen-year-old African American, the news networks
were filled with outbursts of rage intertwined with despair. It still breaks
my heart to recall a young African American man barely holding back
his tears as he exclaimed into a news camera, "We have no hope here!
We have no hope!" But that is not the case for countless reservation
communities. Despite the hardships, there exists a ubiquitous sense of
hope among many Native people, especially among Native educators.
The hope rests in the sense of place, purpose, connection, and identity
offered by tribal cultural traditions.[3] Sitting Bull's vision has not dimmed

because it springs from an undefeated spirit that transcends tribal lines of demarcation. It is a strength of spirit that Native nations share. Likely Alex White Plume, an Oglala Lakota rancher and activist from the Pine Ridge reservation in South Dakota, summarizes the feelings of many Native peoples: "They tried extermination, they tried assimilation, they broke every single treaty they ever made with us . . . They took away our horses. They outlawed our language. Our ceremonies were forbidden . . . Our holy leaders had to go underground for nearly a century . . . And yet our ceremonies survived, our language survived" (Fuller, 2012, p. 48).

## Tribal Strengths

Well over a century ago, Sitting Bull had a specific goal in mind when he pronounced his vision for the future. It is a vision that lies at the heart of this book, namely, the promise of cultural survival and personal perseverance derived from tribal strengths. It is an assurance clearly and unmistakably reflected in Sitting Bull's admonition that "we will retain our beauty and still be Indians." It is the powerful idea that cultural loss does not necessarily need to be the companion of social change.

"Tribal strengths" is the central idea of this book. It is a highly abstract concept that requires careful discussion. Tribal strengths are the sociocultural and social psychological elements that provide steadfast, sustaining power for a nation as well as for an individual. It is important to bear in mind that tribal strengths include both a collective dimension as well as an individual dimension. That is, there are two vital conceptual levels of abstraction to consider in regard to tribal strengths, one sociocultural and the other social psychological.

Tribal strengths derive from a nation's sociocultural history. This specific dimension of tribal strengths is a nation's *tribal legacy.* Tribal legacy serves to define a Native nation and endows the people with an enduring cultural heritage and includes the history, cultural heritage (i.e., customs, traditions, ceremonies, etc.), values, worldview, cosmology, and language of a tribal nation. Tribal legacy, therefore, relates to the historically cumulated culture of a people and thus exists separate from an individual person because the elements constituting a culture are the property of the entire tribal nation. Thought of this way, tribal strengths derived from a robust tribal legacy empower a nation to maintain its cultural distinctiveness against deliberate assimilationist assaults as well as inevitable social change.

While tribal strengths arises from a nation's tribal legacy, ultimately it finds expression in the lives of individual people. Thus, there is a social psychological aspect of tribal strengths. This specific dimension is an individual's *tribal identity*. The concept of tribal identity includes the self-definition and self-confidence a person gains from appropriating his/her tribal legacy. For an individual, the notion of tribal strengths has two fundamental components: one has to do with self-concept, whereas the other relates to self-assurance. An individual may rely on the enduring power of the tribal legacy of the nation to craft and anchor his/her personal self-definition. That self-definition includes a salient value system and worldview grounded in one's greater tribal legacy. A strong self-definition also allows a person to gain the personal confidence, emotional confidence, and even academic confidence to engage the mainstream of American life (including formal education) on its own cultural terms without fear of becoming culturally transformed. Ultimately, tribal identity empowers a person to effectively function in mainstream and tribal societies by providing a strong self-definition and sense of purpose (Huffman, 2008).

It is helpful to think of tribal strengths as a keystone. In the construction of an arch, the keystone is the large wedge-shaped stone at the top that locks the other stones in place; it provides the strength the other stones require for support. With tribal strengths supplying the support, there is a symbiotic relationship between a nation's tribal legacy and an individual's tribal identity. The tribal identity adopted by an individual cannot exist in the absence of the tribal legacy of the nation, but at the same time, the tribal legacy of the nation will not long endure if not kept alive in the heart, minds, and life of the individual, that is, in a person's tribal identity. The tribal strengths held by both the nation and the individual bind them together. Thus, the idea of tribal strengths involves a nation's resilience and endurance derived from a tribal legacy that ultimately finds expression in a person's tribal identity.

In some respects, tribal strengths is to Indigenous peoples what "cultural capital" is to the majority population in a given society. French sociologist Pierre Bourdieu (1977, 1986) introduced the concept of cultural capital as part of his cultural reproduction theory. For Bourdieu, cultural capital includes noneconomic social assets that facilitate success in school settings. These assets include intellect, style of dress and speech, even physical appearance. Most important elements of cultural capital, however, involve the knowledge, skills, and attitudes passed along by parents to children (Bourdieu, 1986; Bourdieu & Passeron, 1990). These forms of cultural capital allow socially privileged students to navigate through educational systems more efficiently than those who do not possess such advantages. Moreover, Bourdieu asserts that because students with cultural capital better understand (and physically resemble) the normative expectations of the dominant society, mainstream educators are more likely to see these students in a positive light and reward them accordingly.

While Bourdieu's notion of cultural capital allows for a degree of understanding of the educational success among middle- and upper-class individuals, it presents difficulties as an explanation for minority and lower-class students' academic experiences. Namely, some challenge the notion of cultural capital as a form of cultural deficit theorizing (Bennett, 2011; Guillory, 1993). In this regard, Tara Yosso (2005) argues, "Bourdieu's theoretical insight about how a hierarchical society reproduces itself has often been interpreted as a way to explain why the academic and social outcomes of People of Color are significantly lower than the outcomes of Whites. The assumption follows that People of Color 'lack' the social and cultural capital required for social mobility. As a result, schools most often work from this assumption in structuring ways to help 'disadvantaged' students whose race and class background has left them lacking necessary knowledge, social skills, abilities, and cultural capital" (p. 70).

These criticisms notwithstanding, the concept of cultural capital does help us understand that hidden cultural assets work in favor of some social groups and against others. However, the notion of tribal strengths also helps us understand that American Indian peoples have their own powerful cultural assets that have sustained them through ages of cultural assaults. In this sense the idea of tribal strengths is akin to Yosso's conception of community cultural wealth, which "focuses on and learns from the array of cultural knowledge, skills, abilities and contacts possessed by socially marginalized groups that often go unrecognized and unacknowledged" (2005, p. 69). Community cultural wealth consists of six types of capital: Aspirational capital involves the capacity to maintain hope for the future even in the face of serious barriers. Linguistic capital includes the intellectual and social skills derived from having experience in more than one language and/or communication style. Familial capital involves the cultural knowledge cultivated among kinship relations that provides a sense of history, memory, and even cultural intuition. Social capital refers to the networks of social relationships and community resources a person can draw on. Navigational capital includes the skills required to maneuver though mainstream social institutions. Resistant capital refers to the knowledge and skills necessary to challenge inequality and work toward social justice.

While the concepts of tribal strengths and community cultural wealth possess similarities, namely, they involve various forms of cultural assets, there are conceptual differences between these two theoretical constructs. The essential difference is that community cultural wealth is conceptualized as assets found in six specific sources available to US minorities, whereas the notion of tribal strengths is conceived as a framework to specifically understand the resilience and endurance of Native nations and individuals in the United States. For this reason tribal strengths emphasizes the importance of a nation's tribal historical cultural heritage as a sustaining force more prominently than is found in community cultural wealth. Likewise, tribal strengths also stresses the importance of self-definition and self-confidence in a more concentrated manner than Yosso's community cultural wealth construct. The social psychological aspects of community cultural wealth are certainly important (as Yosso clearly acknowledges). However, these phenomena do not rest at the center of her theoretical focus.

Ultimately, Yosso seeks to explain how a variety of cultural resources work to the practical benefit of minorities. In this regard, she emphasizes specific instrumental functions of community cultural wealth in ways not found in the conceptualization of tribal strengths. For instance, Yosso regards linguistic capital as an advantage a person gains from being bilingual or having more than one communicative skill. Likewise, social capital includes a network of "social contacts [that] can provide both instrumental and emotional support to navigate through society's institutions" (2005, p. 79). While she recognizes the emotional support associated with social networks, again Yosso stresses the instrumental, practical advantages that can result from simply having social contacts: "For example, drawing on social contacts and community resources may help a student identify and attain a college scholarship" (p. 79). This focus is, of course, consistent with her theoretical point of concealed cultural assets—concealed, that is, from the recognition of many dominant societal members.

In contrast, the notion of tribal strengths is concerned with the everyday life of the individual social actor as well as the enduring vitality of the tribe. Thus, the concept of tribal strengths relates to the social psychological security derived when a person appropriates a sense of identity and purpose from the specific cultural heritage held by the tribal nation. Even in the context of social and family relations, the idea of tribal strengths takes us in a different theoretical direction than does community cultural wealth. Rather than stressing the practical advantages gained from having social networks, the conceptualization of tribal strengths leads us to understand that these social and family relations serve to culturally locate an individual within his/her tribal nation as well as within the larger American society. In so doing, these relations provide emotional security. Seen in this way, tribal strengths is a more general and abstract concept compared with community cultural wealth.

## The Research Effort

In the spring of 2010 I began a series of conversations with twenty-one American Indian educators serving reservation schools in Montana and South Dakota. Initially I was interested in a number of interrelated issues. Namely, I wanted to know more about the roles they regard themselves playing as one of the few professional groups in reservation communities; the challenges they encounter and the rewards they receive; their thoughts on the impacts of No Child Left Behind for reservation schools and students; and their perceptions on tribal identity issues for their students as well as themselves. The result of that first-stage effort is a book entitled *American Indian Educators in Reservation Schools* (2013).

However, the inquiry did not end with the conclusion of the final interview or for that matter with the publication of *American Indian Educators in Reservation Schools*. The aspect of the original research focusing on the tribal identity issues fascinated me. I realized we had only scratched the surface of a complex and intricate web of questions. I needed to engage in further and deeper discussion on this topic. As such, I asked six of the participants if they would be willing to continue the conversation beyond the original research project.[4] Broadly, we decided to discuss tribal strengths, what that means for themselves, and what they believe that means for their students as well as for their schools. All of them readily agreed. There was no hesitancy or reluctance on their part to invest further time and energy in more research. They come from three reservations: two located in Montana and one in South Dakota. For purposes of anonymity, I do not identify the reservations in this book, nor do I identify the participants. I refer to them by pseudonyms.

The South Dakota educators are all Lakota. In fact, South Dakota includes a number of large Lakota reservations. As such, I identify the South Dakota educators by their tribal nationality but not their specific reservation. Montana is much more tribally diverse than South Dakota. Since all the participants are tribally enrolled members of the reservation where they serve, to identify the Montana educators by tribal nationality would run the risk of identifying their reservation. As such, whereas I freely refer to the South Dakota educators as Lakota, I do not identify the tribal nationalities of the Montana educators.

Four women and two men with over 106 combined years of teaching experience, they are the living embodiments of the vision so long ago articulated by Sitting Bull. They all are registered members of the reservation in which serve, and all have spent the majority of their lives there. They have deep roots in their communities and a profound love for the children they educate.

It is impossible to capture the entirety of a person in a few paragraphs. There is too much to tell regarding the richness of their individual life journeys. What I offer here is merely a snapshot of the essence of these six Native educators.

### JUSTIN

Affable, reflective, intelligent, and highly articulate, at thirty-two years old Justin has ten years' experience as an elementary school teacher. Justin grew up on the Montana reservation in which he teaches and is strongly committed to community development efforts. The child of highly educated parents, Justin enjoyed advantages many of his peers did not have while growing up. Among those advantages was a high value on education instilled by his parents. His preparation for the reservation classroom has been thorough and deliberate, essentially following a traditional path. Justin majored in elementary education and Native American studies as an undergraduate student at a Montana university, beginning a career as an elementary teacher immediately following graduation. His first teaching assignment was in the southwestern United States. During that time he obtained a master of education degree in curriculum and instruction from a major university. After several years in the Southwest, Justin made the decision to return to his home reservation in Montana, where he has been for the past six years. He was motivated specifically by the desire to contribute back to his people through service as an educator. In fact, Justin left a comfortable life in the Southwest to return and serve his home community. He is filled with optimism, but it is an optimism that is tempered with realism regarding the challenges facing the reservation. When I asked him if a person can truly "come home again," he remarked, "Yeah, you can go back home again. I guess they say the more things change the more they stay the same. I see that. Things are different, but it's still [name of reservation]. It's still the same place, mostly. Kids have a lot of the same challenges that we had. More kids are going to college now. It's a good thing to see. It's still home . . . It was a good thing to come back here. It's a tough environment. It's a tough place to teach because we have so many challenges."

While his grandparents had been raised in a tribally traditional manner and spoke the language of their tribe, they were the victims of education's long assimilationist campaign again tribal cultures. His parents, therefore, had little introduction to traditional tribal culture. As a result, Justin had only rudimentary exposure to tribal customs and the language as a child and teenager. Nevertheless, he had always valued the traditions of his people and the shared history of Native peoples. This appreciation led him to make a concentrated effort to not only learn about the customs of his tribe but also to appropriate a personal worldview and value system anchored in tribal philosophy and cosmology. The effort involved an eager search for greater knowledge and understanding. Justin reflected:

> As I've got older I've taken my own interest [in tribal traditions]. I grew up here. My family didn't participate in ceremonies. I went to a few

sweats with my dad. Part of that was because my grandparents were both
Native speakers, but they had bad experiences through education, taught
that their culture was inferior. So they didn't stress the cultural element
to my mother. So, therefore, it wasn't an emphasis in my home. As I got
out of my childhood I made sure that it was something I wanted to learn
about, and so I went out of my way to get a Native American studies
degree just for my own knowledge and information. And through that
I started to participate in the Sun Dance ceremonies. I did four years of
that, going to more sweat lodges, prayers, and more traditional manner,
using sweet grass when I pray. And some of that stuff was in my home
[while growing up], but it wasn't as prevalent as a more traditional Native
American household.

Like the others, Justin is a passionate, dedicated educator. Often
critical of tribal governmental leadership, he holds a clear vision for the
future of the tribe. It is the vision Sitting Bull articulated at the end of
the nineteenth century put into practice in the early twenty-first century.

I wanted to become a teacher because I wanted to work with Indian
kids and teach them the things I was taught, that education is important
and you can improve your life through education. You can improve the
conditions of your family and your community if you are educated. And
it went from something I wanted to do for fun, you know as a way to
stay involved in athletics, to something that had a lot deeper meaning
where impacting my culture in a positive manner. If you are going to
face some of the problems that are in a culture [reservation conditions],
you have to equip kids with the skills that allow them to face those problems and make those kids aware of what they are faced with. Throughout
my career my philosophy has been consistently evolving, and it becomes
a little deeper with each year I teach . . . At first it was because I wanted
to coach sports. When I was growing up, the people who worked at the
schools had a preference for coaching positions, and I wanted to coach
basketball. Then as I started to learn more, it's kind of changed where
that wasn't the priority why I went into education. It became working in
the community, because education is a way to improve the state of the
reservation, the living conditions. If you've got an educated population,
you're going to have more opportunities. So, I started seeing a bigger
picture, I guess, as I got a little bit older and started maturing.

Justin's future plans include even greater service to Native children.
He intends to pursue a doctorate, most likely in curriculum and instruction. Although this will require that he temporarily leave the reservation,
this degree is especially important to his career goals. As Justin explains,

"I want to work on my PhD. But at some point I would come back again . . . One of my goals is to work in administration. I also want to work in curriculum development because I don't think there is enough curriculum designed for Native kids."

I found Justin's earnest devotion and impassioned desire inspirational. Even in the face of vexing challenges, Justin appears to keep his eyes fixed on the possibilities for the reservation, possibilities that for him begin in his classroom. The youngest of the six Native educators, Justin has many more years of service ahead.

### TAMMY

A product of the relocation program of the 1960s, Tammy was born in California. She has lived on the Montana reservation of her tribal membership since age six, when her parents left the urban life of the West Coast and returned home. Tammy graduated from college and entered the classroom at a later stage in life. She began her studies at the local tribal college and completed a bachelor's degree through a private college when she was in her midthirties and during the time when her own children were well along in school. Now at forty-nine years old, Tammy has spent eleven years as a middle school teacher, all on her home reservation. While still teaching full-time, she diligently worked through five summers to complete a master's degree from a state university. It represented a challenge, and she is rightfully proud of the accomplishment.

Tammy has always displayed a love for learning. Likely her intellectual curiosity is largely due to the encouragement of her parents. Although only her mother attended college, both her parents valued education and strove to build inquisitiveness into their children. Tammy recalled, "Every night we had to tell what we did in school and what happened, and we always had to go over world events. 'What did you read today?' 'What about in the paper?' 'What happened here?' So we were always valued for our opinions." Yet, she became very discouraged during her high school years. Although she lived on the reservation, she resided in a town near the border. Nearly half the community's population was non-Indian. While she is obviously an exceptionally intelligent individual, negative educational experiences left her with little desire to continue formal academic pursuits. She recalled the painful encounters with racism during her early years and the small-minded attitudes of some of her teachers. During our conversations she freely talked about the pain she still feels over the racist and prejudicial attitudes of others.

> My parents were on a relocation program when the Bureau of Indian Affairs tried to take Native people off the reservation in the fifties and sixties to relocate them to the cities. My parents were relocated to California . . . That is where I was born . . . I don't remember feeling like I was different in California, perhaps due to all different nationalities living together. But, I remember [being] made to feel like I was different on my own reservation, which is ironic to me. I never felt prejudice until I moved back to Montana. Being a child and followed in the stores like you were going to steal; being sent to the school in town where all the Indians went to; just because of where you lived; people not renting their rental units to your family because you were Indian. The teacher in school who said, "She can't get this problem, let so-and-so show us all how." The government class in high school where all the students were against reservations and I was the only one standing up for my Native people. And all the way up to just a few years ago, here in this very school where I work, another teacher asked me why I thought I shouldn't have to pay state taxes! I could go on and on.

Tammy's motivation for becoming a teacher was born out of a desire to serve the reservation. Not merely satisfied with having a job and earning a paycheck, she emphasized the importance of contributing to the common good. During one of our interview sessions she described her path into the reservation classroom and the reason for her continued service:

> I got married young, at 19, and then had my first child at 21. But I just raised all my kids, and I thought most of these kids around here don't have what I had growing up, two loving parents who provided us a good home. I know what kids go through, but I can't say that I experienced it. I had a good life. And I wanted others to know that you can have a good life, and I raised my kids that way too . . . Well I surely don't do that [stay a teacher] for the money, because with my master's degree I could work for the BIA [Bureau of Indian Affairs] Education Department and make twice as much as what I make now. So that is not what I am in here for. It's nice to get paid, and the benefits, and retirement, of course. But I'd like to think that I make a difference . . . I knew at an early age, that I wanted to make some difference. I didn't really know how. But, to me, to be around kids and try to steer them in a better direction and to be proud of who they are and where they come from is rewarding in a way

that no amount of money can touch. Like a person once said, which is my favorite motto, "If you love your job, you never have to work another day in your life." This is me!

Tammy's background includes a mix of cultural influences. She does not see herself as thoroughly culturally traditional as are some on her reservation. Nevertheless, she highly esteems the values and heritage of the tribe. She is also active in many private and public tribal ceremonies and traditions. Tammy explained, "I have my Indian name. It's my grandmother's name. I went through the ceremonies. Dance, powwows. Growing up we went to powwows. My dad is really, I wouldn't say 'out-there' religious or anything, but he says the outside is his church. We didn't go to church or anything like that, but he is always outside with his animals. And that's his church. He is not really practicing traditional, but he says it's important. And my mom too. It's just seeped into the way we were raised. We went to all the [traditional] celebrations."

Possessing a keen pride in her parents, Tammy continually seeks to emulate their values and cherishes their legacy. At one point in the interviews she related, "I am proud of my family and their accomplishments for our people. My mother served on our tribal board for years. My father was a tribal judge for years, sat on the tribal council and now is the chairman of our illustrious tribe. Both trying to make a difference. I want to be like my parents, but in a different way: through the lives of our future, our babies." It is easy to imagine that Tammy's parents are likely just as proud of her as she is of them.

### BEN

Ben is a muscular former athlete with a sensitive heart who cares deeply for his people and the children under his charge. He is thirty-five and for twelve years has served in reservation schools as teacher, assistant principal, and now as principal of a middle school. A first-generation college graduate, Ben began his career on his home reservation immediately after completing a bachelor's degree in education from a state university in Montana. While working as an educator, Ben also completed a master's degree in education from the same institution. Although frequently challenged and discouraged, Ben has no plans to leave and desires to complete his career of service to his people.

Ben experienced a great number of difficulties while growing up. From the divorce of his parents to academic problems in school and episodes of delinquency, Ben's life has not always been easy. But those experiences motivated Ben to aspire and persevere. What is more, challenging life experiences have left Ben with a special affinity for the reservation children who struggle with their own life difficulties. Reflecting back on his life, Ben said:

> I was born and raised here in [name of community], went to school here; graduated from high school here . . . Got into some trouble when I was a kid . . . I am very appreciative of where I am at right now. You know I have really persevered through a lot of things. Just a ton of things. Experienced "rez life" as they call it at the very core, you know . . . But I think I used a lot of my experiences as a kid growing up as motivation to do well in my life . . . When I was a juvenile, I went through a lot of things. Parents got divorced. I was in some trouble, lots of trouble. Almost got sent places I shouldn't have got sent, and I'm very grateful to be where I'm at, and I think my story is one of trials and sort of tribulations and learning from where I've come from and where I'm going. And I think our students need somebody like myself.

Ben repeatedly referred to the lack of positive role models for Native children. As such, he consciously and carefully conducts himself in ways that communicate positive messages to students. And it is no contrived act. His sincere compassion and love for students was clearly evident to me. Ben explained his motivation for becoming a teacher on the reservation and what being an educator means to him:

> I knew that I had to get a degree, and I knew that was the only way I was going to get out. And I don't mean out as in off the reservation, because I feel Indian people can have a larger impact on Indian people on the reservation, especially if you are from the reservation. So I always figured that some way or another I would come back and do something. So that was my goal; was to come back and offer whatever I had . . . And I knew that the degree was going to get me somewhere in life, and it has proved me right. I knew it was going to. So I got a teaching degree, came back here. Never was any debate about me coming back here. One of the things that our students need more than anything is somebody from within who's successful. Somebody who's not the brightest and the smartest but has worked extremely hard to get where I am.

My interviews with Ben were some of the most emotionally powerful of all the interviews I conducted through the years of this research.

For good reasons too. Ben's reservation and his own middle school have experienced a rash of student suicides in recent years. For the educators on this particular reservation, the cascade of tragedies came raining down like merciless blows on their heads. It left many reeling, and Ben in particular felt emotionally drained. In a moment of vulnerability he confessed that had he understood the heavy emotional costs involved in dealing with student suicides, he would have made a different career choice.

> If I knew what was going to happen [the extent of student suicides], of course nobody knows, if I knew that was going to happen, I wouldn't [have] even touched it [assumed a career as an educator]. I wouldn't have someone walk into my door at eight o'clock in the morning and say "one of our kids is dead" . . . If I would have known that those kinds of things were going to happen, I don't think I would have ever gotten into the business, because those things are extremely difficult to deal with. And even more so with the kids [from his particular community] who have killed themselves. I knew them. I used to manage the pool here for quite a few years, and I knew them when they were just babies growing up, and knew the families. You never want to use the word "prevent" when it comes to suicides. But yeah that's the most difficult, by far, that is extremely hard to deal with those things, because I got to go and meet with the families and go to funerals and all that kind of stuff. I would have never got in a position like this if I was going to have deal with those things.

Ben and I both knew he was speaking from a place of deep sadness and grief. Not long after confiding these thoughts in the interview, Ben was presented with the chance to leave the teaching profession when an opportunity to pursue a different and promising career opened up for him. A career, it should be noted, that would have taken him away from the reservation. But Ben rejected the offer and remained an educator in order to serve the children and families of his reservation. This decision clearly demonstrates his commitment to his people.

By his account, Ben was not exposed to traditional tribal culture in any substantial way even though he grew up on the reservation where he currently serves. His father is non-Indian, and his American Indian mother is not a traditional person. He also had no tribal teaching and orientation from his grandparents. Nevertheless, Ben believes that the answer to the social and personal challenges facing the reservation is to find strength in tribal values, most notable, its spiritual core. Indeed, the need to embrace tribal spirituality was a consistent theme in so many of our conversations. At one point, Ben became very sad and simply said, "I think our kids are lost in some ways. They're searching for some kind of spiritual, higher calling, and they're searching for their identity, they're searching for their culture."

What was striking to me was how forthright Ben was about his own lack of understanding and personal grounding in tribal values, world-view, and spirituality. But that is only part of the story. What was equally evident was that Ben clearly values and desires greater grounding in the tribal legacy of his people. He is a man who is searching for more under-standing and growth. My personal view is that Ben, being the humble man that he is, is likely farther along in appropriating those tribal strengths than he may admit or even recognize.

### DONNA

A seasoned educator, Donna is sixty years old and for the last twenty-seven years has served as an elementary teacher and principal on the South Dakota reservation of her birth. In fact, she currently serves as principal in the same elementary school she attended as a child and still lives in the small, remote community where she was raised. Except for a few years as a young woman, she has spent virtually her entire life around the tiny and culturally traditional village she calls home. No one I inter-viewed has deeper roots in the school and the community than Donna.

Life has often been difficult for Donna. A series of heartbreaks have marked the path of her life's journey. A number of personal tragedies and a serious auto accident that almost took her life means that she carries both the physical and emotional scars of a person who has lived through challenging times. But there is also a recognizable quiet strength to Donna as well. She is soft-spoken, serene, and poised. Donna has endured much, and as a result, those life experiences have made her a sensitive and responsive educator. At the conclusion of our last conversa-tion together I said, "Donna, in twenty-seven years I suppose you've seen just about everything." Reflecting back on her life and experiences as an educator, she softly and ever so gently responded, "Oh, yeah. Happy times, sad times, some things you would never believe." There was a far-away, contemplative look in her eyes as her voice trailed off.

Like so many tribally oriented Native people, Donna did not describe herself as "traditional." Yet, clearly in so many ways she is very integrated in the tribal heritage of her people, and it defines her as a person. From childhood she has participated in traditional ceremonies; she continues to smudge on a daily basis (a practice that involves prayers with the burning of sweet grass or sage grass and fanning the smoke into one's face and body; the ceremony is believed to cleanse the soul while the smoke carries the prayers to the Creator); and she is fluent in the Lakota language. Donna also carries both a non-Indian and a Lakota name, which was given to her in a special honoring ceremony.

One of the striking things about Donna's story is that unlike so many of the other participants, she did not become a teacher because of a driving desire to serve. Rather, Donna became a teacher because it was one of the few jobs available on the reservation. For her, the motivation, at least initially, was one of simple practicality. As she explained, "I got married. I was nineteen and started a family and then when my boys went to school there was nothing to do . . . I found out there's really no job prospects. And I was always involved in JOM boards [community collaborative associations created as part of the Johnson-O'Malley Act to ensure the effective delivery of human services to reservations] and parent committees and this and that. And then I had an opportunity to start taking classes at [the tribal college]. So I did, and I got my bachelor's."

After earning a bachelor's degree in elementary education, Donna then proceeded to obtain two master's degrees. The first was in curriculum and instruction from the local tribal college, and the second, in school administration from a state university in Montana. While a motivation to serve the reservation may not have been the initial reason for becoming a teacher, it certainly is the reason Donna remains in the profession. When talking about the rewards gained from being an educator, she related, "Just being able to give back. I mean this is my community. To help kids succeed. And I know everybody. If I'm not related to them I've taught their families, went to school with the grandparents. And it really helps me because I know everyone. I know where everyone lives."

Well into her third decade of service, Donna has earned the respect and esteem of her colleagues and community. As she considered her life and role as an educator, Donna reflected, "I am very proud of who I am as a Native American and what I have accomplished. And I am here for the kids. That's really who I am." As I see it, Donna is a soft-spoken, traditional woman who embodies the tribal strengths of the Lakota.

RACHEL

Outgoing, fun-loving, and joyous with life, fifty-seven-year-old Rachel has traveled far from her South Dakota reservation during her lifetime. For the past sixteen years she has worked as an elementary teacher in a community with many tribally traditional people. Born on the reservation, her parents moved to California in the early 1960s. Her family was not part of the relocation program of that era; her parents went on their own to find employment. After only a few years they returned to South Dakota and lived in the same area where she now serves as a teacher. Facing the poverty of the reservation (her family had neither electricity nor running water) and limited educational options, her parents made the decision to send Rachel and her siblings to a boarding school located on her home reservation. That particular boarding school has been closed for several decades now. It was an experience Rachel was reluctant to talk about and would only tell me she hated the boarding school. Clearly there is much more to this part of Rachel's story. However, out of respect for her preference for privacy about this time in her life, I did not explore more deeply. After the initial meeting she never again mentioned the boarding school experience in any of our further conversations.

After being in the boarding school for two years, Rachel's parents sent her to back to California to live with an aunt so as to attend school there. She loved this time in her young life. She especially appreciated the diversity of her school and the acceptance she felt from others, including her teachers. However, Rachel dropped out of high school and married at the young age of seventeen. As her husband was in the military, they moved to a variety of duty stations in the United States, providing Rachel with even more exposure to the country. With his enlistment up, Rachel and her husband moved to her reservation where they have lived ever since and raised their children and where Rachel found time to earn a general equivalency diploma.

Similar to Donna, Rachel initially decided to become a teacher because it provided an opportunity for employment. However, she also reasoned that the reservation greatly needed Native people as educators. As such, two motivations combined to lead her to enroll in the tribal college and major in elementary education. These decisions ultimately resulted in a path into the classroom. As Rachel explains, "I took education because I liked working with children and there was such a high turnover rate of teachers here on the reservation that it was just like, we need to have somebody that's from here who will stay here and be with our students."

Also like Donna, Rachel has endured her share of personal tragedies. The sudden loss of her youngest child occasioned deep and debilitating depression that caused her to temporarily step away from the classroom. Afterward, Rachel became very involved in tribal politics and youth ministry and concentrated on raising her four children. With time she yearned to teach again. Rachel made the decision to leave politics, an arena about which she was becoming more and more disillusioned, and returned to the classroom.

Rachel is fluent in Lakota and is very tribally traditional in her personal values and worldview. In fact, Rachel is likely the most tribally traditional individual among the six educators. During our conversations, she consistently brought up the importance of keeping Lakota traditions "alive." Indeed, "alive" was a favorite word as she is keenly aware and deeply concerned about the survival of the Lakota language and tribal traditions. Also, Rachel believes that Native children must appropriate the full strengths of their heritage to be happy and fulfilled individuals. She actively, consistently, and naturally teaches her students using Lakota values and customs. She essentially outlined her philosophy on teaching young Lakota children while describing the class activities that had occurred the day of one of our conversations.

> I said to my class, "We're caretakers. And if we don't teach people this, who's going teach them? How are they going to learn to take care of this earth—that this is all we have? We're connected; we're all connected; we're all connected through the plants, through the trees, through this earth—everything is connected. That's how we are as Native people." So, this morning, just that little talk—we talked about that. I said, "We need to take care of her [the Earth]. Even just saying a prayer of thanks. That's what we need to do; that's our spirituality." And I said, "Especially you kids—we need to take care of you, because you're our wakanyeja; you're our sacred beings; you are our future, and you're what's going to happen down the road. So, we have to take care of you; we have to nurture you; we have to teach you."

Even though Rachel has traveled a great deal and has lived in various parts of the country, the reservation and its people lie at the center of her heart. Always in a playful mood, Rachel giggled, "I've been a rez brat all my life, the majority of my life. I've been gone a few years. My husband wanted to move someplace else, and I said, 'Go ahead [laughs]. I'm not going, I'm a rez brat!' And we've been here ever since." She loves her people. Most important, she loves her tribe's children. I observed Rachel's classroom on several occasions. I have also closely watched her interaction with young students. She not only loves them, but they, just as equally, love her too.

### LORI

Lori is a unique individual and a very special educator. For thirty years this sixty-one-year-old woman has labored and frequently fought for Native children as an elementary teacher, as a principal, and in her current position as cultural integration administrator for the school district. Her entire career has been on the South Dakota reservation of her tribal membership. Lori is one of the most highly respected Native educators in the state. But her career has been marked by clashes and battles over the most appropriate ways to teach American Indian children.

She was a first-generation college graduate, and unlike the other participants, Lori spent the majority of her formative years living off the reservation. Her father held a job in a city far from the reservation of their tribal membership. Yet her parents maintained strong ties to the reservation and proactively provided opportunities for their children to gain exposure and engage Lakota culture and language. Lori, while not fluent, can speak and understand Lakota. In many other respects, Lori's personal experiences also differ from those of the other participants. For a short time she attended a boarding school. Unlike Rachel, Lori's boarding school experience was very positive. Also unique in Lori's narrative is that her parents deliberately attempted to prepare their children to live effectively in both the mainstream and Lakota cultural worlds. As Lori explains,

> Well, I'm Native American. I was raised off the reservation. But besides being raised off the reservation my parents used to bring us to the reservation in the summertime to spend with our grandparents, so we had a lot of the language and the culture as a part of our life. I went to

public school until I was a junior and I wasn't doing well in school. I was unhappy so my parents decided that it would be better if I went to a smaller place. They had gone to school in a boarding school, so I chose to come to [name of boarding school] for my last two years. And I loved it. A lot of people have negative things about boarding schools, but the experience for me was wonderful. One of the things my father used to always stress to us, there were ten of us in our family, and he used to always stress that we need to get an education. And when you do, you need to go back and help the people. His philosophy was that we live in two worlds, and we take the best of both. And so that was my choice.

Education was not her initial choice for a career. But a number of different experiences led Lori to reevaluate her options. She soon found her life's avocation.

I think because I had been raised off the reservation it was easy for me to transition into the college setting. And there were a lot of Native American students there, and we had a good support group. But at that time I was a little bit lost. I didn't want to go into business [as a college major], but did I really want to pursue education? So there were personal things that kind of had me come back to the reservation, and once I got into [the tribal college] I thought this is where I want to be . . . Somewhere down the road I wanted to be a teacher. I remember reading *Helen Keller* and I said, "Gee I want to be a teacher." But as I was going through high school I was drawn to accounting. So I went into business [at a state university], and that was my first preference. And then when I came to the reservation I was working for Head Start, and that's kind of when I decided I can do this. There was a teaching program that was being offered at [the tribal college], and that's when I decided that I did want to get into education and went from there.

Eventually Lori earned a bachelor's degree in elementary education as well as a master of education degree from the local tribal college and an administrative license from a state university. During her three decades of service she has waged numerous battles for Native children. Regarding her professional life Lori said,

I just think I had the natural ability to be a teacher. Like I said there were ten in our family, and I was one of the oldest, just taking care of children was something that I was good at. And when I started to work with Head Start, just watching the kids and the curiosity, I thought I want to be part of getting kids to be curious. I was good at it, and I went on and did very well in the classroom as a teacher. I was recognized for my capability of being a good teacher . . . I won teacher of the year, employee of the month, and those types of things. But I was always bumping heads with the administrators. There was one administrator who was Native American, but the rest were not from the reservation, didn't understand the culture, and were trying to push things that were just not appropriate for Native American learners. And I was always challenging them, and they didn't like it. I didn't like having to challenge them.

She is passionate about the need for more American Indian educators in reservation schools. What is more, she has a strong conviction that Native children need to be grounded in their tribal culture. It is this conviction that drives Lori to ensure that students on her reservation become exposed to the tribal legacy of their people throughout their educational experiences. Her face filled with determination as she remarked,

I think being a Native American empowered me as an administrator that I could lead my teachers in a direction that was good for Native American students. I had the sensitivity because I lived on a reservation, understood the culture, had a little bit of understanding of the language, and the sensitivity of what our students needed. So I felt that I had a lot to offer as a Native American instructional leader . . . We have developed a new curriculum, K through 12, Lakota language curriculum, so I'm trying to figure out how we are going to do that because we don't have enough staff. And I'm thinking about using technology. I really believe that if we want the language to come back, because we have pretty much lost the language, and we've done it for years, have teachers go into the classroom and teach vocabulary, the colors, and these things, and some Lakota phrases. But there's no speakers. So we obviously haven't done it right. I believe immersion is the key, but I also believe that immersion is not always going to be successful in school either. I think that if we want to bring the language back, we get families and say, "If you are interested in learning the language with your children, we will form a partnership." With other resources we have, we could have them teach the language to the families. So that's where I am going with this new position [which strives to integrate Lakota culture into the curriculum] . . . And we have so much technology that I'm thinking that, you know, a teacher could turn on their computer and go to the Lakota language site and there would be a person sitting there saying, "Here's the conversational phrase for the week." Because we have so many teachers not from the reservation that they have no idea what the language should sound like and we are expecting them to teach it. We have a long ways to go yet.

The schools on Lori's reservation may have a long way to go. But with such individuals as Lori working hard to make schools instruments of cultural preservation, the prospects are encouraging.

## Research as Nuanced Conversations

The interviews with the six American Indian educators produced richly textured conversations. They had a lot to say. I had a lot to learn. Ultimately, our conversations revealed four important issues associated with tribal strengths and the reservation classroom. First, they talked at length about their own ethnicity and what it means to be a Native educator on the reservation. For them, being a tribal member from the community created a special and crucial affinity with their students. They possessed connections with students that educators who were not products of the reservation could never match. They regarded themselves as role models and understood the obligations resting on their shoulders; they understood their students see them that way as well. They gained personal empowerment from their tribal strengths. The values, worldview, and traditions of their people sustained them and grounded their identities and sense of purpose. In their estimation, tribal strengths made them better educators.

Second, they offered experienced views on the tribal identities of their students. Their thoughts revealed a mix of optimism and pessimism. To them, many reservation youth appear lost and searching for an identity and a sense of direction. Too often they find those yearnings satisfied by the appropriation of the false (and frequently unhealthy) identities and values hawked by pop culture marketers. But they also recognized and highly esteemed Native youth who embrace the traditions and values of their people. They regard these students as grounded and possessing a personal confidence lacking in so many of their classmates. Indeed, all six educators related that students who are building a personal value system founded on tribal traditions and who possess a strong tribal identity are more likely to achieve academically.

Third, the educators presented their views on tribal strengths and the art and practice of classroom teaching. They shared how tribal strengths can be brought into the classroom and made meaningful for their students. The delight and passion of teaching came through as the conversations highlighted successes in the classroom and pondered possibilities. Yet, they also outlined the significant obstacles—some surprising, some not so surprising—which hinder the effective use of tribal strengths as a teaching resource.

Fourth, they candidly discussed their views about the nature of reservation schools. They recognized the dubious history of schools on the reservation. Many of them, in fact, had their own stories of racist teachers who displayed low expectations for Native students and, for a one, her negative experiences with boarding schools. Nevertheless, they saw encouraging, even inspirational possibilities for schools to serve the reservation. For them, with the right leadership and vision, schools can systemically fortify the tribal strengths of Native students. Moreover, they all agreed that schools can and should make significant contributions toward the preservation of tribal culture and language.

The chapters ahead present the discussions we had over these issues. Each chapter will begin with a brief review of perspectives found in the scholarly literature—the voices of scholars, if you will. An examination of issues important to scholars provides a foundation for the consideration of what was on the minds of the six veteran American Indian educators. Frequently, the perspectives found in the scholarly literature match up with the voices found in the reservation classroom. Sometimes, they do not.

# 2

# Tribal Strengths and American Indian Educators

I think we're really blessed to have something that will give us that courage and that strength. That, to me, is a lesson that I can teach. So I teach these kids. I say, "Never be ashamed of who you are. Always be proud of who you are. When you look in the mirror and you see that little, fat, brown face, be happy."

—RACHEL, South Dakota educator

The contrast in our teaching worlds could hardly be greater: Rachel, a second grade teacher of Lakota children in a traditional community of a South Dakota reservation; me, a professor in a graduate program of a suburban university in the Pacific Northwest. On one of my visits to her school I spent the day following Rachel around, watching her teach her young students, taking lunch surrounded by her seven-year-olds who were initially shy and quiet in my presence yet unexpectedly responded with playfulness to my teasing. After lunch Rachel made me do recess playground duty. This was not an option, mind you; Rachel simply told me I was going to do it. The Lakota children played and laughed like all children do at recess, but there was a cultural uniqueness at work on the playground too. Although the children were obviously enjoying themselves, it was unquestionably the quietest recess I have ever witnessed.[1] Nevertheless, it was still playground duty, and even though I have taught for years in a doctor of education program (generally research methods to prepare educational and other assorted professionals for their dissertations), I am a sociologist by training and have no K through 12 experience of my own to draw from. Doing playground duty with elementary children is not a normal part of my professional activities. There is no use denying it, I felt out of my element.

His name was Jeff, and he was a bundle of boundless mischievous energy. Nothing about Jeff displayed angular regularity either. His teeth seemed to jut in different and odd directions, his hair was cut in uneven lengths all over this head, his shirt was buttoned up in the wrong holes, and if that were not enough, Jeff's eyes were crossed. I quickly learned that Jeff's preferred daily sport was making life miserable for his classmate Judith. Apparently it was an everyday routine in Rachel's class. Jeff would pick on and upset Judith. Judith would tell on Jeff. Jeff would get in trouble with Rachel. Rachel would make Jeff stand against the wall for the first five or ten minutes of recess after lunch. Everyone seemed to understand and accept the order of things—except for me.

On the day I was doing playground duty, Rachel wandered off to talk with another teacher. Likely thinking that even a college professor should be able to handle playground duty, she left me alone to perform my responsibilities. Those duties, I should note, included the obligation of keeping an eye on Jeff and making sure he took his punishment and stayed against the wall. He kept inching around the corner in an effort to light out for freedom. Every few seconds I had to call him back to remain in sight. I realized that Jeff was never going to make the full term of his sentence before he bolted and got into more trouble. So without any authority whatsoever, I pardoned Jeff and told him to go on and play. Unfortunately for me, it turned out that Judith's preferred pastime was making sure Jeff was fully chastised for the abuse he heaped on her each day. As soon as she saw that I had released Jeff from the wall, I heard Judith break the delightful quietude of the playground by yelling at the top of her voice, "Teacher, teacher! That white man just let Jeff go from the wall!" I looked around to see all the Native teachers, including Rachel, staring at me in that remarkable Lakota manner of sanctioning a person without saying a word. Afterward, no one ever said a word about Jeff and the unauthorized parole incident. No one had to.[2]

The episode on the playground and the school day's events surrounding it reveal much to my mind. Taken together, they demonstrate the importance of tribal strengths at work in reservation schools. In large and small ways, in obvious and subtle moments, critically important cultural socialization occurs when tribally grounded Native educators engage and guide Native children. The ways in which Rachel and the other teachers at her school interact, instruct, and, yes, even discipline children are based on tribal principles and values that have an impact far beyond what any standardized test can measure. When American Indian educators draw on their tribal strengths, important and wonderful education occurs. But here is the crux of the matter, and there is no way around it: only tribally grounded Native educators possess those crucial tribal strengths desperately needed by Native children.

American Indian educators who understand and use their tribal strengths are the most important resource in reservation classrooms. But not just any Native educator will do. At our first meeting Ben made an incredible statement that has stayed with me. He said, "You always hear [that] an Indian educator can be more successful with an Indian student, but on the flip side an Indian educator can hurt an Indian student more than a white or non-Native teacher can." He went on to explain that insensitive and uncaring remarks have a greater impact coming from an American Indian educator than from a non-Native educator. He argued that reservation schools must be staffed with compassionate Native teachers and administrators who can convey the values and perspectives important to their peoples. In other words, he argued for American Indian educators who can effectively employ their tribal strengths.

## Perspectives from Scholars

Until recently, scholars paid scant attention to Native educators (Erickson, Terhune, & Ruff, 2008; Huffman, 2013). But that neglect is beginning to change, and a growing number of researchers are increasingly turning needed focus on this critically important group of professionals. In 2010 and 2011, after I conducted research on American Indian educators in reservation schools, I identified two types of educators: "facilitative educators" and "affinitive educators" (Huffman, 2013). Facilitative educators regard their primary role to be an effective and competent educator guiding the learning process so that Native students will be academically prepared for the future. Affinitive educators see their primary responsibility to be a role model for Native students, a person Native youth can look up to and emulate his/her success. I greatly admire the

six educators who offered their voices for this study. They represent
everything special about having the right Native educators serving in the
right situations in reservation schools. Personally caring, professionally
competent, and culturally connected, individuals such as these project
both the facilitative and affinitive dispositions necessary to successfully
educate American Indian children.

Two major themes regarding the contributions of American Indian
educators stand out in the literature. First, researchers have documented
the importance of American Indian educators as a cultural resource to
their people. More specifically, Native educators frequently serve in the
critically important capacity as cultural brokers between their tribal communities and the professional world of mainstream education. Given the
turbulent history of American Indian education, the ability to negotiate
between cultural worlds is invaluable for the future of tribal nations.
Second, Native educators serve as role models for American Indian
youth. Researchers consistently document the importance of Indigenous
educators as providing real-life proof to Native students that success in
two cultural worlds is not only possible but also physically present before
them in the classroom.

### AMERICAN INDIAN EDUCATORS AS CULTURAL RESOURCE

Intuitively it makes sense that American Indian educators are an invaluable resource to reservation communities. They stand in the cultural
crossroads of mainstream and tribal cultures (Beynon, 2008; Cajete,
2006; Huffman, 2013; Leavitt, 1995). Indeed, Canadian scholar Arlene
Stairs (1995) refers to Native educators as "cultural brokers" for their
potential to translate different (and often seemingly incongruent) edu-
cational/cultural methods and goals into meaningful systems and outcomes for Native communities. Yet, despite their obvious importance,
there has been surprisingly little research on the personal and professional experiences of Native educators (Cherubini, 2008; Huffman,
2013). In one of the few such studies, June Beynon (2008) met regu-
larly with ten Canadian First Nations teachers for a decade following
their graduation from the Prince Rupert/Simon Fraser University First
Nations Language and Culture Teacher Education Program. This unique
teacher preparation program included Ts'msyen culture and Sm'algyax
language as fundamental components of the professional training. Basic

to Beynon's study was the attempt to document the transition from being a tribal community member to becoming a Native educator. As Beynon relates, she wanted to "provide insight into their dilemmas and struggles and tell of how they went about taking action to resolve them" (p. 14). One of the frustrations facing First Nations educators is that the new role of teacher initially made them suspect in the eyes of some of their neighbors. Because a legacy of distrust has attached itself to schools in many Native communities, even Native educators are frequently regarded "as allies of the school and alien to their communities" (p. 97). This poses a serious dilemma for Native educators and has been noted by previous researchers as well (Cherubini, 2008; Duquette, 2002). For the participants in her study, Beynon explains,

> teachers occupy positions both in the cultural worlds of their communities and their schools. Within the figured world of their community, teachers participate in a wide range of activities including formal and informal clan, family, and village ceremonial gatherings (e.g., name-giving ceremonies); seasonal activities (e.g., fishing, hunting, and food preserving); public dance and drumming performances; and sports events at home or in other First Nations communities. Within the figured world of school and classroom, they participate in language programs, school-wide assemblies, district and province-wide curriculum initiatives, and conferences, as well as the daily implementation of provincial curriculum in language arts, math, and other curriculum areas. (p. 98)

She continues by explaining that her investigation sought to understand "teachers' dilemmas and delights in the noisy and messy process of constructing positive relations between these two figured worlds" (p. 99). It is noteworthy that the teachers in Beynon's study increasingly drew on their tribal strengths as their careers continued and evolved. Although facing perplexing challenges, these First Nations educators were equipped with the appropriate tribal repertoire to engage the community in culturally consistent and meaningful ways. "As the teachers take the initiative to engage in conversations with parents and other community members, they can draw on ways of communicating that are well rooted in community traditions of learning. Respect is a central tenet in Indigenous pedagogies . . . Through dialogue, teachers begin to chip away at the old authoritative discourse of church and mainstream schools that devalued Indigenous ways of knowing and learning" (pp. 99–100).

These First Nations educators managed to employ the fundamental tribal values of trust and respect in productive ways. Ultimately, tribal strengths enabled them to build bridges with community members. By so doing, they became successful cultural brokers.

Hill, Vaughn, and Brooks Harrison (1995) documented the reliance on tribal strengths among five American Indian female teachers who had, in the authors' words, "been reared by culturally conscious Indian families" (p. 42). The researchers examined the personal journeys of these women and the dilemmas they encountered as they transitioned into the classroom as an educator, several of them after they had raised their own children. Virtually all the women had overcome perplexing and even devastating personal experiences so as to realize the goal of becoming an educator. A specific focus of this study was the use of tribal identity to maintain personal and professional coherence. Ultimately, the authors provide evidence that the reliance on their tribal strengths, tribal identity in particular, facilitated their individual successes and allowed the participants to be effective teachers of Native youth. The authors conclude,

> The participants' personal and professional lives evidence the primacy of Cherokee, Kickapoo, Creek, Chickasaw, and Choctaw women's roles as mother, grandmother, provider, and conduit of tribal traditions in the historically matrilineal tribes . . . American Indian spirituality (focusing on a personal connection to nature and the entire Indian community's needs) is important to each participant . . . After graduating, the women's ethnic identities continued to guide their personal and professional lives . . . It seems that integration of their ethnic identities with the larger culture has contributed to the participants' triumphs over adolescent and post-adolescent periods of self-doubt and depression. (p. 48)

A Canadian study conducted by Kitchen, Cherubini, Trudeau, and Hodson (2009) utilized a unique and culturally consistent methodological approach to gain understanding on the professional experiences and challenges faced by First Nations educators.[3] Over three days, six beginning First Nations teachers attended a retreat and participated in a talking circle facilitated by a Native elder and a Native researcher. Additional researchers, both Native and non-Native, rounded out the research team and assisted in the data organization and analyses. Their collaborative work revealed richly nuanced insights on the experiences of the educators. Specifically, five important themes emerged. The first theme related to their teacher training and induction into the profession. Generally, the participants reported that their teacher training programs did not adequately prepare them for teaching First Nations youth. They regarded their preparation as Eurocentric with little attention on the actual teaching of Native students. Moreover, they also felt undervalued as First Nations educators, and some reported disturbing accounts of discrimination and racism from their non-Native peers. One of the participants said, "They don't treat you as a teacher. You're just an Indian teacher"[4] (p. 362).

The second theme included what the authors refer to as "facing the realities of Aboriginal students and communities" (p. 363). The educators faced perplexing challenges dealing with the personal and social struggles facing Native peoples. As one of the participants succinctly related, "Educating our youth is a really tough job"[5] (p. 363). Nevertheless, the First Nations educators profiled by Kitchen et al. retained their optimism for the future of their communities and students. The authors report, "Although these challenges caused by colonization are daunting, the tenor of the discussion did not remain negative for long. Such comments were soon followed by laughter as they recalled the joys of teaching. Through sharing and healing the pain soon turned to determination and hope" (p. 363).

The third theme related to issues of self-identity and cultural identity for both their students as well as themselves. The First Nations educators focused on the need to work toward enhancing the positive cultural identities of their students. Significantly, this effort resulted in the greater examination of their own cultural self-identities. What is more, they reported tensions resulting from serving as a role model to Native students, on the one hand, while also feeling compelled to establish their own acceptable cultural identities in the eyes of the community.[6] The need and desire to teach tribal languages was the fourth theme voiced by the participants. They realized the enormity of language loss facing their tribes. While only two of the six individuals were fluent in their tribal language, all felt a great responsibility to help their students and communities preserve the language. They keenly understood that the tribal language is a major contributing factor to the uniqueness of their people and includes the very essence of their culture.

As the fifth theme, the educators articulated the need to teach tribal culture. Although closely related to the necessity to teach the tribal language, the theme also includes the expertise and knowledge required to convey the history, traditions, and deep values of the tribe. The desire to teach tribal culture posed tremendous frustrations for the participants. Specifically, they felt restricted by the Eurocentric curriculum imposed on them that left little room to realistically integrate and engage their tribal culture in the classroom. As one teacher explained, "We're Native people teaching a non-Native curriculum to our people. We're not Native people teaching about us within our own curriculum" (p. 367). Nevertheless, they embraced the notion that meaningful cultural teaching could be an important step toward recuperation from the historical damage done to their communities. The authors observe, "Culture and cultural identity emerged time and again as central to Aboriginal education that engaged students, connected them to their language and culture, and contributed to healing and development within Aboriginal communities. It was evident that they envisioned the teaching of Aboriginal culture as extending beyond teaching material culture to bringing to life social, cognitive, and linguistic culture" (p. 367).

These findings reveal the complexities in becoming a cultural broker for Native teachers. But they also underscore the potential benefits for tribal communities in having such cultural brokers as a resource. Nevertheless, Native educators encounter a myriad of issues. Prominent among those issues are challenges in transitioning from being a community member to the role of professional educator in the community, dealing with the social and personal problems facing Native communities, maintaining a strong personal tribal identity, and shortcomings in their professional training and current curriculum to respond to the cultural needs of their students and community. The research reported in the literature also makes clear that Native educators rely on their tribal strengths to meet these challenges. Researchers consistently report the resilience and determination common among Indigenous educational professionals (Cherubini, Niemczyk, Hodson, & McGean, 2010; Cleary & Peacock, 1998; Duquette, 2002; McCarty, 2002; Swisher & Tippeconnic, 1999; Writer & Oesterreich, 2011).

Not surprisingly, the six American Indian educators I interviewed derived tremendous métier from their tribal strengths as well. Their tribal strengths provide a sense of identity and purpose in life as individuals. But what is more, they related that they gain professional efficacy directly from their tribal strengths. Indeed, they took care to explain why they are more effective educators because of their tribal strengths.

### AMERICAN INDIAN EDUCATORS AS ROLE MODELS

In his novel *Pudd'nhead Wilson,* Mark Twain wrote, "Few things are harder to put up with than the annoyance of a good example." While we can all likely identify with that observation to some extent, it can also be said few influences are more enduring than the impact of a teacher's example on a young person's life. There is a small but growing body of literature documenting the importance of American Indian educators as role models in the lives of Native students (Huffman, 2013). In the highly influential book *Collected Wisdom,* Linda Miller Cleary and Thomas Peacock (1998) report their research with sixty Native and non-Native teachers of American Indian students. Cleary and Peacock found pervasive examples of the potent impact culturally competent and professionally successful American Indian educators have on students' educational and life experiences. They report, "Many of the American Indian teachers we interviewed are successful examples of individuals who are grounded in their tribal cultures and able to function successfully in majority society" (p. 111). These educators stand out as living examples of success in two cultural worlds.

There appears to be a keen appreciation of the responsibility to serve as a role model among Native educators. Although there is not a great deal of literature on American Indian educators, the importance of serving as a role model for Native students nonetheless appears as a consistent theme in the published studies. For instance, Brock University professor Lorenzo Cherubini and his colleagues have conducted a number of research investigations on the professional experiences of Canadian First Nations teachers (Cherubini, 2008; Cherubini, Kitchen, & Trudeau, 2009; Cherubini et al., 2010; Kitchen et al., 2009). Most of these studies have involved emerging teachers and reveal important insights. For instance, their extended research efforts have documented that Native educators are motivated by a desire to help preserve their tribal cultures. This mission is not only noble but also provides encouraging news for efforts toward tribal revitalization. Additionally, the educators specifically identified their responsibility to serve as a role model for First Nations youth.

Similarly, in a study of First Nations educators, Friesen and Orr (1998) reported that their participants described a number of important responsibilities they should perform as professional educators of Native students. These obligations included helping to preserve tribal culture, working to build First Nations communities, and serving as a role model to Native students. What is also intriguing in this particular study is that many of the participants suggested that both their career choice and the desire to work to preserve tribal cultures were heavily influenced by the role models from their own youth. Most notable in this regard were their own First Nations educators.[7] Not only do American Indian and First Nations educators generally recognize the need to serve as a role model for students, but evidence also suggests that Native students want their Native teachers and principals to serve as role models (Martinez, 2014). Smith-Mohamed (1998) found that having educators as role models was much more important to Native students than it was for non-Native students. Cleary and Peacock (1998) also reported that American Indian children respond positively to the effective role modeling presented by Native educators. What is more, research has revealed some indirect links between the lack of role models in schools and American Indian academic attrition. A classic study conducted by Donna Deyhle (1994) revealed that school leavers cited the absence of positive influences provided by American Indian educators (more to the point, the absence of American Indian educators in their schools) as a major reason why they dropped out.[8] Their decisions to leave school stand as testimony to the importance of having visible, positive professional and cultural role models in the classroom.

## Voices from the Reservation

The perceptions held by the educators in this study are remarkably consistent with previous research findings. Their experiences lend support to the conclusions offered by so many others on the critical importance of culturally and professionally effective American Indian educators in reservation schools. The participants recognized the cultural importance they represent to their communities. They regarded themselves as cultural brokers standing at the crossroads of tribal and mainstream societies. Because of their cultural positioning, they can also serve as effective role models.

But there is more to their perceptions and experiences. They specifically wanted me to understand they are not only cultural brokers for their communities or even role models to their students but also possess a special and unique affinity with Native students. It is an affinity emerging from their shared tribal legacy and tribal identity. Indeed, it was virtually impossible for the educators to talk about serving as a role model without also discussing their cultural affinity with students.

Additionally, the participants clearly gained tremendous personal and professional strength from their tribal legacy and identity. Tribal strengths empowered them both as private individuals and as educational professionals. Normative behaviors and conduct, worldviews and values, spirituality and cosmology are largely shaped by the larger tribal legacy and work to form their tribal identities as individuals. What is more, their voices give evidence of the how these tribal strengths ultimately endow their professional efficacy as Native educators to Native students.

## PERSONAL AFFINITY, ROLE MODELING, AND TRIBAL STRENGTHS

At the end of the school year, Donna was presented with a surprise. Due to forecasted district budget cuts and last-minute turnover at another school, she was asked to assume the duties as principal of a second school. As such, she would be required to split her time and energy between two schools, one an elementary school, the other a small combined elementary/middle school. Much like her present assignment, the additional school also served a tribally traditional community in a remote location on the reservation. As the schools were culturally similar and rather close (at least by rural South Dakota standards), the district considered the joint assignment a reasonable request. Donna, being the professional that she is, accepted the added responsibility and saw it as a yet another opportunity to serve more Native children. As she explained the steps she took toward assuming her added duties, Donna made an intriguing comment:

> When I found out at the end of the year that I was going to be going down there, I went down and introduced myself. Of course it's seventh and eighth graders and they were checking me out and the girls were

kind of a little snippy about it. But this one boy asked me, he said, "Why do they always change principals down here?" And I said, "I don't know." Then I said, "The reason I'm coming down here is because there are budget cuts." So I explained the budget cuts, and I explained the whole thing. He said, "Well, are you going to stay?" And I said, "Yes." And he said, "How are you going to do that?" because he knew I was still a principal here. So I just told him, "I'm not going to neglect either school. I'm going to give it my best." And then the very next question that the students asked me was if I was Indian. And I said, "Yes." And they asked lots of questions like, "Have you ever been to a sweat?" And I said, "Yes." And they asked, "Do you have an Indian name?" And I said, "Yes." And they asked me if I have ever been to different ceremonies and if we did the Flag Song at my school.[9] After that it was okay . . . Every single one of us here at the school participates in ceremonies and speaks some of the language. Until you fully understand and know you who are, you won't get beyond it [connect fully with Native children]. You won't.

Donna's affinity with reservation children and her ability to serve as a role model are naturally associated with her tribal strengths. There is nothing contrived in these attributes, and it is clearly evident in the simple way she described her transition to serving as the principal of the second school. I asked if her ethnicity is a strength that assists her as an educator. Donna responded by saying,

I think it does. You know, for the non-Indian teachers that come in, I mean, it's hard for them to understand who we are. Our school, it's more culturally based. We take the students as we get them and we go from there . . . And I mean, everyone has a part in it, the bus drivers, the cooks . . . Because they care. I mean, they know who these kids are, they've lived the life that the students live. Every one of them. Some of them were raised going without just as much as these kids, so they relate more. Plus with their families . . . I just have this perception, because I've lived this long and I know. I think for the most part Native teachers that are in the school system, they do understand our kids. They do understand our kids. I can name some instances at [name of a different reservation school] with non-Native teachers, they could care less. They think if they put up pictures of Native Americans they're integrating the culture. Stuff like that, but I mean it's just—but since there are so few of us, it's hard to change people's ways.

Like the others, Justin too believed that serving as a role model is a necessary part of serving American Indian students. Additionally, possessing an affinity with students provides a natural opportunity to teach traditional tribal values and ways. Justin related,

> They [the students] need to have good role models to learn from; they can watch them and see how they do things. Then they can do those things with practice, with guidance. There's too much drama and instability in the homes, and the kids see that. They see conflict and then they come to school and that's what you have; you have conflict. You have girls who can't get along with each other and boys who want to fight each other. That's what's going on in those homes. In a way, that's becoming part of the modern Indian culture—that struggle, those bad things that destroy homes and destroy people. Even if I don't talk to them about what I'm trying to teach them as traditional values, that's what I am doing. I have that character-building based on traditional values in mind. People with good, strong character. I need to do that. That's another common thing about most Natives is they called themselves "the human beings," or "the people," and what that meant, in my understanding, was just a humble person with a good character, but also be willing to stand up and say something when it's time to stand up and say something. If you have to defend your home, they defended their home as best they could. A lot of those people, people like Crazy Horse, got killed. A lot of those people who were leaders ended up not getting a pass on everything that they could have passed on. Some of the kids who were potentially going to carry those values went to boarding schools, and they were ashamed of themselves when they were done. They didn't want to be Indian, they wanted to change or they didn't want to talk about it anymore. I think you've got to get back to that mindset of what it means to be an Indian; not 50 years ago, but what did it meant to be an Indian 200 years ago. It's a tough thing to do. Individuals and communities have to figure out how to implement it.

The notion that Native educators have a deeper understanding of the needs of Native children and the community compared with non-Native educators repeatedly emerged from the interviews. Justin reflected, "There's benefits to being from here and working here. I was able to fig-ure out what happened, what was missing, what was lost. Then you see people who have aspects of that, you can see which families are doing a job of raising their kids to be respectful. I think when I've talked to parents, they've said things like, 'Well, we tell them to listen to you. We tell them you're from here, and you went to school and you came back.' I think the parents recognize that . . . I think the parents, the older people recognize it. They know that I'm from here, and they understand that

I'm trying to do something here. People have been working on the same thing that I'm working on, but we don't have enough."

Rachel, echoing the sentiments voiced by Donna and Justin, also believes that American Indian educators have inherent advantages over non-Native educators (and perhaps even some less culturally traditional Native educators). In her estimation, they stand out as important role models for American Indian students. She related,

> I think it helps our children around here more because we do identify and we do want our kids to succeed. We do live that value; they are our future. We want them to succeed. And a lot of our teachers on the reservation that aren't from around here, they don't have that connection. They don't have that identity. They don't have the resources to build on . . . A lot of these teachers don't have that. They don't. And it's like they have these—they have a structure set for them that, "That's the way it has to be." The kids have to be this way and teaching has to be this way . . . I think we do have an advantage with the kids here. Not all, because some of our teachers that are Native American still see the old school way that they were taught and they teach that way too. So, it's not all of us . . . But because we're here and we understand and we can pass [tribal strengths] on to students. And that's why I said the other teachers don't have that experience; they don't know that.

Tammy framed this same notion in slightly different terms. For her, tribal strengths not only give her greater understanding of Native children but also directly contribute to her professionalism as an educator. In effect, the tribal strengths she possesses involve an essential part of her efficacy as a teacher. This perspective is revealed in her thoughts on how she disciplines Native students and attempts to form personal relations consistent with tribal values.

> Well, to me, being here, I live here, being brought up here. I'm not going nowhere. A lot of teachers don't live here. Or, they might be here for a couple years and move on. I'm not saying that's wrong, it's just that I'm here. I'm not going nowhere. Of course I'm going to try my best even more because of that. After hours you could see me too. It's not just during from eight to four. They see me at six. They see me on the weekends. They see me mulling around with my family. So, I think that—and being professional—they don't see my name in the paper doing things I shouldn't be doing. [Laughs] Hopefully. Ever. Knock on wood. [Laughs] And, to me, that's a professional. And, I treat my fellow teachers how I want to be treated—with respect. If I don't like what students are doing,

I don't yell at them. Or, I don't embarrass them. I might put my hand on their shoulder and go, "No, you don't do that," and later, "I want to talk to you." Tell them why. I don't have to bring what they did out in front of everybody to try to shame them. I wasn't brought up that way. My parents would say, "Okay, no, we don't do that." I think being professional, all of us should act that way, especially in front of these kids out here. We shouldn't yell at them. It just drives me crazy, you know, when other teachers are yelling. It's like, "Why? You're just wasting energy. You're going to have a coronary if you keep this up. Just calm down." [Laughs] "Be nice and calm, and then we'll talk about it." But don't go off the handle for every little thing. To me, that's the best way to act professional. Treat each other how you want to be treated. If you have a disagreement, and everybody does—I don't get along with everybody here. I try to, but I don't shun them. We just get along as best we can.

Ben provided some of the most intriguing thoughts on this subject. Ben's personal background was filled with cultural ambiguity, a dilemma that is still a persistent tension in his life. With tremendous candor and not a little vulnerability, he discussed difficulties with the cultural ambiguities in his life. "I ain't a [tribal] traditionalist. I don't follow Christianity. I never grew up with any of that stuff. And as I search for it [tribal traditions], I don't know where to go. I don't know what to do. I don't know who to reach out to. I raise my kids to be respectful, come to school ready to learn, but that road [appropriating tribal culture] for me being a father has been a struggle. There's very few people in the community who you can go up to and say, 'What do I do? Help me raise my kids.'" Yet Ben also related his deep admiration for the Native educators who are grounded in their tribal strengths. It is this grounding that in Ben's estimation makes them superior educators and widely respected by Native students.

What I have found is, if you've lived the life of one of our students, then you should understand where they come from, what they're bringing to school. But that doesn't always happen. If our teachers had a better understanding of culture, it would make them better teachers. We have a few teachers in the building that actually are traditional and understand the religion, lived the religion, practiced the religion and the cultures. The few teachers that we have that are like that and are in touch are the ones the kids know how they feel. Not only do those teachers understand, we look to them for guidance, I guess you could say. We look to them as a sort of in-house spiritual leader. And I think if all of our teachers—you don't have to live that life and you don't have to be an expert—but if all of our teachers had that base, including myself, I personally think you'd see an astounding turnaround because there's just something there that you can feel. It's just, you know, when you're in the presence of someone who has that cultural base. There's almost a nobility about them or something. If we all sort of strive for that, I think our kids will feel it; they'll feel it; the kids will feel it; we'll feel it; and it's hard to explain. It's really hard to explain, but you know who they are; they know that they're traditionalists. You know that they incorporate the culture. And for them it's a natural incorporation into the instruction. But there's only a few. And if we had more teachers who were more tuned into that I think it'd make a big difference . . . You know who those people are, and there's just something about them. Kids know who they are, and there's just something. If all of our teachers had that—it's not really a magical thing, but you just—you know they're traditionals. You know that the respect that you give them is higher. The kids know this. It's just like when an elderly guy walks in the building, kids tend to change. They know they have to be respectful, they know that they have to adhere to rules. And they treat him different than they treat teachers. And it's the same thing with the few [tribally oriented teachers] that we have in the building. The kids treat them differently because they're more respected.

Clearly the participants recognized the importance of their personal affinity with reservation students and understood their potential as role models. What is more, they believed that being a Native educator on the reservation empowers their professional efficacy. But they also wanted me to understand why that is the case. For them, personal strength, which includes professional efficacy, results from drawing on their tribal heritage and identity.

### PERSONAL EMPOWERMENT, PROFESSIONAL EFFICACY, AND TRIBAL STRENGTHS

"Are we connected? I think so. I told them [her second grade students]. I said, 'Gee, fat, brown face.' [Laughs] I said, 'Well, some of you guys have got little, round faces.' But as long as they're told that [to be proud of their tribal identity], eventually, that's going be part of them. 'Be proud of who you are; don't let nobody make you feel bad about who you are.' That can go for anybody, too—across the board, for anybody; any race." Leave it to Rachel to describe the importance of tribal identity in her own unique way. For Rachel, as well as the other educators in this study, tribal identity is the key to their own as well as their students' well-being and success.

The educators spoke of the personal strengths derived from their tribal identity and heritage in a variety of ways. For some, such as Tammy, Donna, Rachel, and Lori, their tribal strengths simply emerged as a result of their early cultural socialization. As a result, they expressed tribal values and worldviews naturally and organically. For Justin, the strength resulting from tribal heritage and identity was deeply personal and involved a great deal of effort to appropriate and continually cultivate. He spoke freely of his cultural journey and the results that have ensued.

> I think from everything I've gathered, and from some of my professors at the university, I was able to identify, or find a part of, myself, that was connected to my ancestors that I didn't have growing up. Growing up here I was missing that connection. But through some people I have met I have gained. [Name of an American Indian university professor] is probably the most influential one. She taught the religion class at the university. There was a religion class, and there was two other classes I took from her, but she was probably the most influential in connecting me to those traditional values and understanding this is the way things used to be. This is what we should be working to try to bring back, certain behaviors, the cooperation, and taking care of the least before we take care of the person who has the most. That used to be what the culture was about. One of the stories she was talking about was the person who was the richest was the person who had the least because they gave everything away. They took care of everybody else. But everybody had the most respect for that person. That respect that the person was able to gain by being a generous human being was more valuable than any possessions. You don't see a lot of that anymore. I mean, you can't do that completely in a modern society, but you could do more than we are doing. We could do more than we are doing.

One of the most esteemed and experienced educators among the participants, Lori reasoned that a greater awareness and acceptance of one's tribal heritage and identity has benefits beyond personal grounding. If American Indian educators possess this kind of understanding about their own tribal legacy and who they are as Native individuals, they will be poised to make greater contributions to the education of Native children. As she explained,

You have to know who you are before you relate to someone else. That's what I'm doing with this cultural proficiency book [a teaching manual on Lakota culture she was constructing]. It's all about learning about what culture is, first of all, and then knowing about all the different types of cultural proficiency and culture competency and knowing that your background is different also. A lot of our people don't think of it that way. They don't realize, like, why do I do the certain things that I do and why do I believe the things that I do in the classroom? So it's teaching. What we're trying to do is teach all of our teachers to be aware of who they are and what they contribute in the classroom from their culture and then teaching them that sensitivity of other people's cultures and how that all works in an organization. It is important that we know who we are, first of all, what our background, what our cultural background is, and how we become sensitive to someone else's culture. Because by being sensitive then there's things that you can do differently in the classroom.

## Crazy Horse's Soliloquy and American Indian Educators

Dying from a deep stab wound in his back, Crazy Horse uttered his final words to the few individuals huddled in a dimly lit, stuffy cabin room.[10] In his simple soliloquy, Crazy Horse lamented, "We preferred our own way of living" (Vanderwerth, 1971). It was a melancholy yet defiant declaration.

Cultural survival requires stubbornness. Even in her playful way, Rachel's instruction to her young students encourages the stubbornness necessary to resist negative racial stereotypes: "I think we're really blessed to have something that will give us that courage and that strength. That, to me, is a lesson that I can teach. So I teach these kids. I say, 'Never be ashamed of who you are. Always be proud of who you are. When you look in the mirror and see that little, fat, brown face, be happy.'"

Happiness, lament, pride, stubbornness, defiance—they are all ingredients of cultural survival. They are also part of the experiences of the six American Indian educators. These teachers all felt the personal burden to lead their students toward cultural survival by using the natural affinity between them. They also understood the power of their personal example and how the intentional, calculated use of their own tribal strengths is important in order to unveil the potential of the tribal strengths within their students.

The educators in this study would surely identify with the sentiment found in Crazy Horse's dying words. Their perceptions provide not a hint of the culturally assimilationist philosophy that so long dominated educational thought and practice. They find their mission, their passion, and their purpose within their tribal heritage and identity. They prefer their own way of living.

# 3

# Tribal Strengths and American Indian Students

I belong to a unique set of people who are survivors! We are still here. I love being Native!

—Montana middle school student responding to the question, "What does it mean to be American Indian?"

It takes no small amount of courage to teach middle school students. Tammy has the necessary courage and a lot more too. On one of my visits to her class, I wanted to know what her students believe it means to be American Indian. So I asked.[1] When you ask a group of middle school kids a question, it is hard to tell what answers you might get in return. In this case most of the responses revealed just how important the question was for this class of young Native students. They generally appeared to deeply consider what to say, with several writing down their responses before responding verbally. The seriousness of the answers underscored the significance of the question. The themes surrounded notions of relatives, history, and respect. Consider a few of the typical responses.

Being Native to me means that I am proud of who I am and who my relatives are. My family means so much to me. I love my grandparents who take care of me. They try to teach us all about our traditions and to live in a good way. I hope I can do this for my own kids someday. We go to celebrations, and it is good to be with other tribes. I think the main thing is to respect each other and all the living things. Otherwise we won't have much left. Being Native means to honor our living and our dead.

Being Native means to me going to powwows and going to sweats and honor our loved ones that have passed away and respect our elders and other people. Native means to me that I won't be called anything else but Native or Indian and that we have big families that care for us. Being Native means everything to me. Being Native makes me happy and glad because I'm just like everyone else.

Being Native means being proud of being from a group of people who were here in the land before anyone else. We lived with the animals and all living things with respect. We only ate what we had to. We didn't cause harm to our mother who takes care of us who is called Earth. We hunted and used all the animal parts and [did] not waste any part of it. With hides we made our homes and clothes. The meat we ate. The bones we used as tools. I think that it must have been a hard life but a good one. We should try to go back to some of the old ways. But I think I will miss my iPod!

Perhaps the most powerful comment was offered by a young girl who simply said, "I belong to a unique set of people who are survivors! We are still here. I love being Native." Although the majority of the students provided thoughtful responses, I wish I could say that all the students in the class that day articulated such clear and decisive feelings about being a Native person. Some were quiet and a few flippant (they were middle schoolers after all). Later conversations with Tammy revealed her concerns over the cultural ambivalence of some of her students. She explained, "Honestly, most of them really know who they are. They don't have deep, deep roots. I wish they would know more about their ethnicity. They know who they are. They know what tribe they are, they know where they're from, but it's not deep rooted. This is on the surface. So we try to bring that out more. We do respect our elders and what they say. But it's not so much what I say, I think. It's how I act. Because kids, they know if you're a fake or not."

The conversations with Tammy and the other educators regarding American Indian students remind me of a discussion I had with a Native woman some twenty years or so ago. When conducting interviews with American Indian students attending a predominately non-Indian college, one of those students, a middle-aged student, related an account of her preparation to go to college.[2] Just before she left the Cheyenne River reservation of South Dakota, an older woman, considered one of the tribe's elders, took her aside and recounted a story of two little sisters. According to the student,

> She told me about the little girl, two little girls that were playing outside, and one had a red dress on and the other had a blue dress on. And they were playing hide-and-seek, and their father told them not to go too far, you know, or not to hide where they can't be found. But they kept on playing and didn't pay too much attention to what he was saying. So it was the little girl in the red dress, it was her turn to hide, so she went to hide. But she went off too far. And her sister in the blue dress went to find her, but she couldn't find her. She looked all over the place, and she couldn't find her sister. So she started to get scared, and she called for her but she wouldn't answer. So she ran back and told her father, and he went out and her mother she went out to look for her. They spent two days looking for her. Finally they gave up on her. Then one day not too long after that her father was out hunting. He was walking along the river and he looked up and on top of the bluff he could see something waving on a shelf of a cliff. So he climbed to the top of the bluff, and there he found the little girl's red dress in an eagle's nest, and all that was left was her bones and part of her red dress.

This sad tale is a metaphor, a warning to the student. As she explained, "My grandmother was warning me not to go too far, to be careful and not forget where I come from, or I might lose who I am." The story is an obvious caution against the dangers of assimilation. What is remarkable, as well as disconcerting, is that the elder needed to make this counsel at all late in the twentieth century. Yet, it is undeniable that for scores of American Indian students, both at precollege and college levels, mainstream education has necessarily been regarded with concern as a potential threat to one's ethnic identity.

The story of the sisters told by the college student and the exercise among the Montana middle school students on what it means to be American Indian go to the heart of an important issue, namely, concerns over the tribal identity of Native students. Discussion on the nature of tribal identity for American Indian students has been a favorite topic for a long time among scholars of American Indian education studies. The concept itself is referred to by different names—cultural identity, ethnic identity, native identity. In my own work, I have previously referred to the idea interchangeably as cultural identity or ethnic identity (Huffman, 2001, 2008, 2010). However, here I use the term "tribal identity."

As explained in chapter 1, the reason for the deliberate use of this label is because I have a specific theoretical notion in mind. Tribal identity is the social psychological dimension of tribal strengths and refers to an affinity with and appropriation of the cultural attributes and historical heritage of one's tribal nation. I prefer the term "tribal identity" because it replaces a generic conception of an individual as "Indian" (e.g., cultural or ethnic identity) and instead locates the person as a member of a specific nation and owner of a unique cultural legacy. In this conception, the tribal strengths offered by a particular American Indian nation or nations (as is the case for those with multiple tribal heritages) are potentially the inheritance of any member who claims them for himself/herself. Additionally, it is critical to reemphasize that tribal identity is conceptualized as providing the self-definition and self-confidence needed to function effectively in both tribal and mainstream contexts. While these processes are important for anyone, they are especially crucial for Native young people.

## Perspectives from Scholars

The nature of the academic experience for American Indian students has been an area of examination among scholars for a long time. There are so many themes on this topic in the literature that it is difficult to know where to begin. The literature can be overwhelming. Yet, with that said, when it comes to the tribal strengths for Native students, two areas of scholarly focus tend to stand out. First, researchers have offered considerable discussion on the challenges in forming a tribal identity for American Indian students. Second, they have produced numerous examinations on the connection between a person's tribal identity and academic achievement. This latter consideration in particular has been the basis of a great deal of debate, disagreement, and contradiction among scholars.

### TRIBAL IDENTITY OF AMERICAN INDIAN STUDENTS

All young people seek and need a personal identity. Eminent psychologist Erik Erikson (1950, 1963, 1968, 1980) spent a major part of his career attempting to understand the developmental dynamics associated with crafting a personal identity. Erikson argued that failure to achieve a fully developed identity during adolescence could lead to an identity crisis. The term "identity crisis" has since become part of popular culture nomenclature, frequently used with comedic overtones. For Erikson, however, identity crisis involves a state in which the individual is incapable of facing adulthood with emotional and psychological confidence and security.

Much of the subsequent work on the identity development for adolescents built on Erikson's seminal theoretical effort. For instance, identity status theory is especially helpful in understanding identity formation among adolescents (Marcia, 1966, 1980). I should note here that the basic premise and fundamental assumptions of identity status theory are generally consistent with the way in which tribal identity (as an important dimension of tribal strengths) is theoretically conceptualized. Thus, this theory holds potential in understanding the identity formation challenges facing Native youth.

Incorporating Erikson's concept of identity crisis, identity status theory asserts adolescents continually search, test, and reevaluate the core aspects of their identity, namely, their personal values, attitudes, relationships, and self-definitions. As such, adolescents alternate between conditions of identity crisis and identity commitment. More specifically, identity status theory regards an individual's identity as involving four potentially different statuses during the course of maturation (Marcia, 1966, 1980). It is important to understand that these statuses are psychological stations in life, not a series of sequential stages. Thus a person can, and does, move in and out of the various statuses until one status becomes more or less dominant in adulthood. The first status is referred to as "identity diffusion" and is a state in which the adolescent does not possess a secure sense of values, attitudes, relationships, and self-definition. As such, the youth is not willing or capable of committing to a specific personal identity. In "identity foreclosure," the second status, the adolescent is willing to conform to the values and attitudes expected from others, such as those imposed by parents or peers. "Identity moratorium," the third status, involves a crisis in which the adolescent actively explores various values, attitudes, relationship choices, and self-definition but has not committed to any set of ideals. It is notable that in the context of identity status theory, a crisis is simply a time when an individual is willing to critically evaluate his/her values and beliefs.

An identity crisis does not necessarily involve a traumatic episode in a person's life (although it well could). Finally, the fourth status, "identity achievement," includes a condition in which the adolescent has gone through a crisis and subsequently can truly commit to values, attitudes, relationships, and self-definition that provide a consistent, stable personal identity. Ultimately a well-developed identity achievement status offers the person a sense of his/her strengths, weaknesses, and unique distinctiveness (Hardy & Kisling, 2006; Kroger, Martinussen, & Marcia, 2010; Marcia, 1966, 1980; Marcia, Waterman, Matteson, Archer, & Orlofsky, 1993).

Scholarly work on identity development of adolescents, such as that offered by identity status theorists, has consequently expanded to the issue of ethnic identity development. As difficult as personal identity formation may be for nonminority youth, given the added racial and/ or ethnic component, scholars regard identity development as even more complex for minority youth (Ogbu, 1978, 1981, 1987, 2003; Phinney, 1989, 1990, 2000; Tajfel, 1978, 1981). For instance, minority adolescents frequently must contend with identity formation pressures from both in-groups and out-groups (Ogbu, 1987; Tajfel, 1978, 1981). This is the basis for the so-called acting white dilemma for many minority youth and especially for African American young people[3] (Buck, 2010; Fryer, 2006). Yet, for minority youth, the development of a strong sense of ethnic identity is fundamental for healthy self-esteem, emotional security, and racial/ethnic pride (French, Seidman, Allen, & Aber, 2006; Rowley, Sellers, Chavous, & Smith, 1998; Toomey & Umaña-Taylor, 2012; Umaña-Taylor, 2011).

Tribal identity for Native youth is especially critical as it serves to personalize one's ethnicity and locates the individual socially, culturally, emotionally, and perhaps even spiritually. It is hard to conceive of any aspect of the maturation process more powerful than the development of one's very identity for a Native young person (Cleary & Peacock, 1998; Stiffman et al., 2007; Werito, 2013).

The development of a tribal identity for Native youth can be enormously complex. Native youth are increasingly required to locate their identities in a local-tribal context, a national context, as well as part of Indigenous peoples of the world and, thus, a global context. As a result, Carol Markstrom (2010) asserts that tribal identity must be understood as forming and operating within at least three conceptual levels: the local level, the national level, and the global level. She argues that any conceptualization of tribal identity which ignores the intricate emotional, social, cultural, and political complexity that contextualizes its development is seriously misguided. As such, she identifies what she considers the three salient levels that provide a framework for understanding tribal identity development among today's American Indian adolescents. As Markstrom explains:

> The local level . . . encompasses, in part, knowledge and understanding of one's group, experience, actions, and choices . . . There are currently 564 federally recognized tribes and numerous other bands and tribes encompassing an array of languages and customs. Therefore, more general themes apparent across various cultures are addressed, but specific illustrations are interspersed to bring substance and specificity. In addition to identity formation at the local level, American Indian adolescents must negotiate the complexities of living i n the broader and influential national context of U.S. society . . . Social contextual influences on identity also occur according to the less physically proximal global level . . . [G]lobalization has contributed to growing indigenous rights and identity movements that bridge across first-peoples worldwide. Hence, the global level is centered on indigenous youth of the world. (p. 520)

This complicated process may be filled with tremendously beneficial rewards and opportunities, but it is also fraught with perplexing challenges. Indeed, Vincent Werito (2013) refers to the process by which Native youth must establish and maintain a tribal identity as "negotiating the multiple and contested terrain of identity" (p. 58). Regardless of its complexity, just as a strong ethnic identity is important to all minority young people, tribal identity specifically is vital to the sense of security, emotional well-being, and healthy growth for Native youth. Among other benefits, research evidence demonstrates that a strong tribal identity is connected to positive self-esteem, feelings of belonging, a sense of purpose in life, and a lesser chance of substance use and abuse (Herman-Stahl, Spencer, Aaroe, & Duncan, 2003; Huffman, 2011; Kenyon & Carter, 2011; Kulis, Napoli, & Marsiglia, 2002; Marsiglia, Kulis, & Hecht, 2001). Moreover, a number of studies also report that the spirituality derived from one's tribal identity is an especially salient factor in preventing suicide attempts among American Indian young people

(Garoutte et al., 2003; Hill, 2009; Johnson & Tomren, 1999). Notable in this regard is the sense of community and a feeling of belonging associated with a strong tribal identity[4] (Kenyon & Carter, 2011).

### TRIBAL IDENTITY AND ACADEMIC ACHIEVEMENT

Researchers have expended much effort attempting to ascertain how the tribal identity of Native students is related to their educational experiences. Not surprisingly, the assumed connection reflects the prevailing social attitudes of the time. When assimilationist assumptions dominated scholarly thinking, researchers generally reported that a strong tribal identity among American Indian students was associated with academic difficulties (Berry, 1968; Miller, 1971; Scott, 1986). More recent scholars typically regard a strong tribal identity as facilitating educational success (Davis, 1992; Horse, 2005; Huffman, Sill, & Brokenleg, 1986; Okagaki, Helling, & Bingham, 2009; White Shield, 2009).

Many scholars treat the issue as an either-or scenario, that is, a strong tribal identity is either associated with academic failure or a strong tribal identity is related to academic success. However, a closer look at the findings reported in the literature reveals a more complex picture. Ironically, a strong tribal identity is connected to academic difficulties for some Native students, and at the same time, it is connected to educational achievement for others. Thus, the relationship between a strong tribal identity and educational success and lack of success is not an issue of either-or but rather one of being both. For instance, in a quantitative study involving 1,607 American Indian and white middle and high school students, James, Chavez, Beauvais, Edwards, and Oetting (1995) operated from essentially assimilationist assumptions. They presented their working hypothesis by declaring, "It seems reasonable that Indian students with relatively high Euro-American cultural identity should succeed better in, and be less likely to leave, mainstream schools than those with relatively low Euro-American cultural identity" (p. 185). Yet they found that Native students embracing either a strong "Euro-American" cultural identity or a strong "Indian" cultural identity were less likely to leave school and more likely to do well academically. It was those students who displayed a weak affinity with any cultural identity who were more vulnerable to academic difficulties. Their findings suggest that ambiguity in one's cultural identity is the real difficulty in realizing academic success. Thus, the critical variable was simply holding a strong cultural identity (whether Euro-American or American Indian) for their sample of students. Comparing their results with past research, the authors appear somewhat puzzled and concluded by offering two likelihoods: "Thus, we have two alternate possibilities from past research: that higher levels of Indian cultural identity will have a negative relationship to school success, while higher levels of non-Indian cultural identity will have positive relationship to it; or that both types of cultural identity will have positive relationships to school success" (p. 186).

As the James et al. study was quantitative, the authors had little basis to understand the complex reasons that may account for this pattern in the data. I was fortunate enough to have an opportunity to conduct a qualitative study spanning five years and involving an unusually large sample of sixty-nine American Indian students attending a predominately non-Indian university (Huffman, 2001, 2008). The major focus of this study was to understand how tribal identity is associated with the college experience. I found virtually all students possessing a strong affinity and identification with traditional tribal culture experienced a great deal of alienation and frustration with the mainstream college. However, in time they tended to divide into two groups. One group refused to surrender their tribal identity and assimilate to what they (not unreasonably) regarded as the mainstream cultural mandates of the university. Typically, this group left the college soon after their arrival on campus. Few rarely stayed more than two or three semesters. I referred to this group as "estranged students" because of their severe alienation from the university. For many of these individuals, the decision to leave college was a cultural survival strategy. While some dropped out of college because of academic difficulties, a significant number left the university as a way to resist forces they saw as culturally assimilationist and thus a threat to their tribal identity.

The second group also did not desire to assimilate to the mainstream. However, unlike the estranged students, they dug deep into the strengths offered by their cultural background and, in so doing, forged a strong tribal identity. This identity eventually created a sense of confidence and self-assuredness that allowed them to engage the university on its own terms without fear of personal assimilation. In effect, they were able to move across and between cultural worlds because their cultural repertoire of skills and knowledge had been broadened. The key point here is that they did not surrender any of their tribal cultural skills and knowledge, they simply added new cultural abilities. I referred to these students as "transculturated students." This group, rather than leaving college as a means to protect their tribal identity, used their tribal identity to facilitate their academic goals,—that is, they used their tribal identity as a source of confidence and as an anchor for their values, orientation, and purpose. As a result, most of them had successful college experiences.

The point here is that a strong tribal identity combined with a salient tribal cultural orientation is actually related to both academic attrition as well as academic achievement. The outcome largely depends on how an individual regards and uses his/her personal tribal identity. With this realization, a growing number of scholars and practitioners are working toward ways in which Native students can utilize their tribal strengths and tribal identity as a means to gain educational success. A good example of this is the Success Academy created as a joint effort by the Flandreau Indian School of Flandreau, South Dakota, and South Dakota State University.[5] Essentially, Success Academy was designed to introduce Native students to the world of higher education. It held as a goal the preparation of not merely some but all of its students for postsecondary education (Lee, 2013). But the initiative did not stop there. It also sought to educate the academy, in this case South Dakota State University, on the unique needs of Native students. A major focus of the effort included ways in which the university and its staff would reorient itself to honor and affirm the tribal identities of Native students. MaryJo Benton Lee of South Dakota State University, one of the primary founders of Success Academy, offers this description of the initiative: "What occurred through the birth of Success Academy was a reorganization of the culture of schooling at two institutions. What occurred was systematic change. At the Flandreau Indian School that has meant the adoption of a comprehensive school reform model aimed at preparing all students for postsecondary education. At South Dakota State University this reorganization has involved developing ways in which American Indian identity is affirmed, honored, and incorporated into the institution's culture" (p. 30).

According to Lee, the combined efforts of the Flandreau Indian School and South Dakota State University have met with impressive success.

After twelve years of cooperation, the program could count among its accomplishments a greatly enhanced high school graduation rate, a general boost in high school academic achievement, increased numbers of students enrolling in college, building the capacity of South Dakota State University's effectiveness in serving American Indian students, creating a more diverse university campus, and strengthening the American Indian community at South Dakota State University. Lee also reports that the effort served to affirm and honor American Indian identity into all aspects of the university. She contends, "Programs like Success Academy are a way for the institution to rethink how best to work with American Indians. To succeed, Native students should not have to leave their identities parked outside the university gates. Rather the university needs to develop a broad range of programs, activities, events, and curricula that celebrate Indian ways of life" (p. 155).

## Voices from the Reservation Classroom

Undeniably, tribal identity is one of the most crucial factors to consider in the education of Native students. I wanted to explore this issue with the six veteran American Indian educators and hear their perceptions surrounding the tribal identity of their students. It turned out they had much to say on this topic. Generally, the discussion centered around two themes. First, the educators articulated what they considered to be the prevailing tribal identity issues facing their students. There was no shortage of concern over these issues. Second, they contended that students' tribal identity is an especially powerful dimension of tribal strengths. They were convinced that a strong tribal identity will not only bring academic rewards but also is essential to prepare Native students for success in life.

### TRIBAL IDENTITY ISSUES AND CONCERNS

Regarding the tribal identity of reservation students, perhaps Justin best summarized the general perception among the educators when he remarked, "You got kids from homes where they're from a group that is maintaining the culture and has been able to preserve some things, and then some kids don't really know hardly anything about their culture . . . I think a lot of these kids with a strong identity, their Indian identity comes from home. I don't know that in our community there's a whole lot of discussion or dialogue about what it means to be an Indian person." The educators saw tremendous complexity and variation among their students regarding their personal identities. Some students hold a strong personal tribal identity, and the educators were optimistic about them and their future. But many others do not possess a strong tribal identity, and clearly the educators were concerned about these students. According to the participants, a significant number of their students, perhaps the largest group, know who they are racially but lack real cultural depth, and thus they are left dealing with ambiguity. All the educators mentioned that these students seem to be looking for direction but are frustrated by the lack of guidance. Then there are those students who are simply ambivalent about a tribal identity. Many of these students have turned to other identities, such as gang affiliation or hip-hop culture, as a way to define their lives and values. There are also young people who seem not only to have rejected a tribal identity but also actually parrot many of the more common negative stereotypes of American Indians. Thus, based on the interviews with these educators, Native students are arrayed along a range of dispositions toward their tribal identity.

While the educators recognized that many of their students possess a strong tribal identity, they were concerned for the majority of their students. They perceived a great deal of tribal identity ambiguity among the young people of their reservations. A lack of cultural depth was a consistent theme during our conversations. Like a number of the educators, Justin pointed out that superficial aspects of tribal culture have become normative among many reservation people, yet students in his estimation also need to appreciate more substantial tribal values and beliefs. He reflected, "There's kind of a modern cultural identity is how I would see it. Then you have kids that grow up and they don't have any experiences with their traditional culture . . . They might say things like going to powwows, going to sweats, going to Native American church, the activities, going-around dances, feasts. They'd probably mostly talk about the activities that they recognize as part of their culture. I'm not too sure that many of them would say the values, and talk about the values. They know they're Indians. But as far as knowing what that means, some of them would have a better understanding than others." Corresponding to the absence of cultural depth, the general loss of tribal culture concerned the educators. Lori spoke specifically to the issue of cultural loss and its impact on the tribal identity of students:

> You know, we've got to instill those values or go back to those values that were so important to us and teach and model it to our young people, and I think that's where we're at right now . . . We're almost to the point where we're losing our language completely. And in our schools we're also losing the culture. Our students don't have much of a tribal identity anymore because there's no language left. Hardly at all; you don't hear the language being spoken. There's a lot of surface stuff that's done in the schools, but not the deep culture. So I don't think our students know who they are as tribal members. So we're struggling now to try to bring that back into the schools . . . I really think that our students have lost that identity. The whole reservation, I think, is struggling. We met last year several times with the tribal members of our reservation through the college, through the Tribal Education Department, and we had committees, subcommittees. One that was just going to deal with the language, one that was just going to deal with the culture, and one with the history. And we were using the staff at the college to do the historical part of it. But it was so overwhelming for everybody. It was like, they didn't know where to begin because we know that the language is almost gone. So we had good, deep discussions about it. They want the schools to teach the language, but who do the students go home and speak it to? Because there are no speakers in the home anymore. They don't hear it in the community.

The educators identified the absence of cultural guidance on the reservation as a serious issue. Indeed, all six of them referred to the lack of teaching on the tribal legacy of their people. For some this involved a concern over the aging of traditional people who are fluent in the tribal language and few younger people to replace them. Others were concerned about what they regarded as the general ambivalence toward traditional culture and language pervasive on the reservation. Justin talked at length about his distress over the lack of cultural guidance for his students.

> It's kind of sad, you know? We've been assimilated enough that the identities, unless you go out and find it, nobody's going to give it to you. You've got to go get it on your own. I hope to bring some of that to these guys. It's a tough thing to do, especially if you've got kids who are like, it's not a priority of theirs. It's either got to be ingrained, or when you're older it will become a point of interest, or something that will motivate them to learn about themselves and where they're from. I don't know

if just our community is like that or if it's something common across Native communities. I would think we have a shared history. We're all different cultures, but our commonality is we have a shared history. That assimilation, those boarding schools, they took a lot out of Indian people. Indian people didn't want to be Indian people because they were taught they were lesser human beings. I think that oppressive mentality is something. Indian people went through traumatic experiences. Even if our generation isn't going through that, we feel the effects of it. Before there's any healing and before things start to get back to that sacred circle of life, before that gets healed, it needs to be understood. And right now I don't think that in Indian country it is completely understood. It's understood by some individuals, but as a culture and as a whole, it's not.

Ben identified a number of interconnected issues when he talked about the lack of cultural guidance. His comments had an urgency that reflected the recent tragedies which had befallen his school and reservation. With tremendous passion he said,

We have some kids whose families do lead a very traditional lifestyle. And the thing that we find is it works good if you get kids who know the language and the customs and the culture. And with that comes the respect and all those character traits . . . The expectation is the school is going to teach them their language, which is part of our responsibility, but it's not all of our responsibility . . . with the culture and the traditions comes a spiritual base, comes this idea of right from wrong, this idea of treating your parents and your grandparents the way that they should be treated. But it doesn't happen a lot. Right now we're sort of a community living in fear. I think every day we live in fear. We have a lot of drama in the community, but we don't have anything that our kids can call their own in terms of culture and traditions . . . I still think that the fear of us having and needing the culture and having the identity and raising our kids with the language and everything is something that we need. But I don't think we know how to get there. I don't think we know because it's been so long. There's not a lot of people left anymore that are tied to the culture. I think it's a missing link in all of that.

Even among students who do understand the need for a tribal identity, the educators perceived a lack of depth in their cultural understanding. Tammy acknowledged as much when we asked her middle schools students what it means to be a Native person. Tammy realized that while her students recognize their ethnic identity, the identity itself does not necessarily impact their lives due to the lack of substantial cultural meaning.

As noted at the beginning of this chapter, her observation is a powerful one, "Honestly, most of them really know who they are [racially]. They don't have deep, deep roots [lack cultural grounding]. I wish they would know more about their ethnicity."

Four of the educators, Justin, Ben, Tammy, and Lori, lamented the appropriation of other cultural identities among some of their students. In particular the appeal of hip-hop culture and, more menacingly, youth gangs compete with tribal identity among students hungry for a sense of self and direction in life. In Lori's view, the reservation is presented with a challenge. She saw a real desire to revive the culture, but serious barriers stand in the way. Much of the challenge connects directly to the rival identities that compete to define reservation youth. As she put it,

> You know, families want to learn the language, along with their child. We go into the communities. You're going to start slow, but maybe slowly it will build and it will build and pretty soon we'll hear the language again. And I think that's kind of the drive of the reservation now is to try to get the language back and the culture back. So there are more cultural activities that are happening in the community. But our youth have chosen a different culture, and it's the hip-hop or all the other cultures that they see in the media and stuff. They don't have that pride anymore. We had a speaker speak to our staff at the beginning of the year, one of our traditional Native American resource people. We did a video of him and we asked, "What is it that you want the schools to do?" He said we made the mistake of forgetting these important things like the values that we live by. He said that's what our children need. So, yeah, I think it's so, so crucial that we start talking to our kids and having them understand historically what has happened to our tribe, to our people, and where we are now and where we want to go. We need to understand what the barriers are and why there's been such a cultural breakdown. We need to understand why people have turned to different cultures because they didn't have that identity. And now the media is out there, so there's so much for them to grab onto. I was at a presentation last week. We were talking about the Lakota language and I said, 'When you walk down the streets you don't hear a lot of English with these young kids.' You know? Not good English. You don't hear the Lakota language. You hear a different language, and it's all the hip-hop and that type of stuff that you're hearing out there.

Justin and Ben voiced concern over the negative side of the alternative identities adopted by some of their reservations' young people. Justin commented on the cultural inconsistency between some to the adverse values espoused within certain aspects of hip-hop culture and traditional values of his tribe. With a great deal of perception and wisdom he related,

> I don't think that these kids know where they're from. They don't know why they're here. Their textbooks don't teach them that. Their textbooks are from a Eurocentric point of view. That's something that I try to correct. We started talking about it and I showed them a map that was all Native people, and I said, "When do you think this map is from?" They're fifth graders. They aren't going to know everything, but some of them were saying 1900s, 1800s. They didn't understand that 1491 is a significant date. They don't understand that they're from people that have this rich history and culture. They don't know about it. So they end up adopting aspects of the mainstream. And a lot of it they pick up on are negative things. There's a gravitation towards hip-hop culture. Some hip-hop has a positive message, but a lot of hip-hop is about degrading females and being dramatic, trying to establish yourself as the big dog. Those are things that go against the traditional cultural values where people are trying to take care of everybody else as opposed to using other people as a stepping stone for their own status. That's what's taken over because their culture isn't there right now.

Ben had more to say on this subject than any of the other participants. With unblinking honesty, he outlined the nature, complexity, and danger of a gang identity replacing a tribal identity for Native youth. Of special concern to him is the acceptance of negative stereotypes of American Indians by some students.

> We've been concerned about gangs and communities of gangs for a number of years because we knew our kids weren't attached to their culture, identity, where they came from. And we knew that a lot of parents didn't live that life. And it gets to the spirituality end of things. A lot of our parents with Native kids, there is very little of that traditional sense of upbringing. And I think it's primarily because somewhere along the line we lost it. I didn't have it in my life growing up. A lot of our kids here don't have it. So what's happened the last four or five years is we have seen a real increase in the amount of gangs. A lot of gangs. And, of course, we knew that was going to happen. We knew it was coming because these kids don't have anything to call their own. They don't have anything to steer them in the right direction. And that's what the identity, culture identity would provide for them. I think they're proud of a lot of the history. But I think somewhere within there, things change and being proud of who you are turns into sort of, "Yes, I'm proud of who

I am, but I really don't know who I am. I'm proud of being an Indian."
Then along with that, "Well, what is an Indian?" Nowadays you ask a kid
what an Indian is, he might tell you, "It's someone who sits on the street
and gets drunk" because we have so many of them. They might tell you,
"It's someone who abuses grandparents and parents and girlfriends and
wives." They might tell you, "It's someone who doesn't work." There's a
whole wide range. But I think the crux of the issue is they are proud of
who they are. I think they are. I think there's a lot of history and a lot of
tradition there that makes them who they are. I don't think they would
want to be anyone else. But in the same breath, I don't know if they
know who they are.

Ever the optimist, Lori saw opportunity in the challenge presented by
cultural loss. She believed that pressing social and personal difficulties
are causing people on the reservation to appreciate the value of their
tribal strengths. As she explained, "You know, living on the reservation is
a struggle. It's survival because of the poverty. So much of that has gotten
in the way that they've lost a lot of our culture. People are starting to
talk about what happened. I think it made people wake up and say, 'You
know we're not doing something right.' Now I think they're realizing
that."

### ESSENTIALITY OF TRIBAL IDENTITY

The educators value a strong tribal identity in their students but see
few who possess such an identity. They believe a strong tribal identity
supplies students with a solid and spiritual foundation, a coherent
worldview, and a sense of purpose and direction. Justin, Ben, and Lori
even mentioned that possessing a strong tribal identity, and in particular
embracing the spiritual significance of that identity, is an essential part
of the solution to the social problems confronting reservations. As Ben
put it, "I think the culture, the identity, I think it's a definite cure to a
lot of the issues that we have. One thing you notice right away is those
kids whose parents have raised them traditionally and have a lot of the
culture are good families. They dance, they attend powwows, and there's
very few of them, but they're good families. Their kids are always really
respectful, good kids. They just seem to be happier. They just seem to
have a sense of where they're going, not just kind of floundering. And I
think it goes with spirituality because a big part of our culture and who
we are is spirituality."

Justin voiced a view almost identical to Ben's. He too believed that holding a strong tribal identity is associated with a strong value system. Like Ben, Justin also has confidence that students possessing a tribal identity will make significant contributions to the community. "You see people who have traditional culture. You can see which families are doing a job of raising their kids to be respectful. Even some families, their skin is lighter but their behaviors are more in tune with a traditional worldview. You put the others before yourself, there's that self-sacrifice, and then things take care of themselves. The kids are taught to observe, and listen, and learn, and not to be disagreeable, and to have self-control. They're the ones who are more likely to go somewhere and do something, and then hopefully, bring something back here."

All six of the educators contended that students possessing a strong tribal identity do better academically than those Native students lacking a strong tribal identity. Confidence, self-assuredness, and a salient value system work together to enable the student to engage and achieve in school. But all those attributes derive from a strong sense of their tribal identities. Justin went even further to argue that students with a strong tribal identity and who rely on the tribal legacy of their people are better equipped to take control of their futures and resist many of the social problems besetting their communities. He asserted,

I think they need that awareness. It goes into that self-identity, who you are, where you come from. It gives you a certain amount of pride. You take pride in being a Native American. There's a race of people that was almost exterminated. It's a tragic history. All these kids don't understand that they're from a group of survivors, human beings who have survived a cultural assault. You understand that you're coming from those people, it makes you want to do more. You don't want to be a victim. You want to take control of your own destiny and your own future. You establish that confidence and then you can realize that these drugs and all these problems that we have here, it's not who we're supposed to be. It's kind of like us continuing that oppression, that state of mind. Then you fall into victimhood. Then you're blaming everyone for the problems and not realizing that if things are going to change, the people have to take control and change them. If you want to make a better life for the next generation, then the generations who are in control need to be changing things. A lot of it is values. There's a lot of values that go with the culture that have gone by the wayside. I think the kids that do have that cultural grounding, they have something more that some of the other kids who don't have it. There's that culture that they have; it's not just an identity, but maybe it is a strong value system.

The two educators from more traditional communities, Donna and Rachel, did not evidence the same level of concern over the tribal identity issues of their students as the educators from less traditional communities. Donna, for instance, regarded the tribal identity of students as a natural product of their rearing and socialization. She did not see struggles with tribal identity among her students but also acknowledged that students from less traditional districts of the reservation do not have the same cultural continuity as the families served by her school. As she recounted, "It [tribal identity] is embedded. I mean, my students that come here, I don't really think of it as an issue for us. Because that's the way we're raised. I mean, we know who we are already, so to me in this area it's not an issue. But in the other districts when I go to the other schools, it is an issue. Because some of the students, they weren't raised in a traditional sense. Culture is who we are, that's the only way we were raised." Rachel, however, pointed out that there must be consistency and authenticity when modeling and teaching reservation youth. She noted, "They have a strong identity; identify real strong with the songs—the Flag Song. And even here, they have the Flag Song in the morning . . . I think they have to have that connectedness. They have to have that part of themselves. I think you can read it out of a book and say, 'Okay, I'm teaching you generosity. How to be generous.' But if you don't live that way of life, it's hard for you to teach it. I think it's really important that they have that grasp of who they are."

Nevertheless, Rachel also recognized the difficulties culturally traditional students face once they leave the community and go beyond the reservation to college. Often at the mainstream college, students do not have a sustaining, nurturing support system. As a result, some students become discouraged and leave campus for the more welcoming setting of home. As Rachel recounts:

> I still think cultural grounding is important. It may or may not help them academically. It depends where they're at because every place else doesn't nurture that [a tribal identity]. The [tribal] college here nurtures that; our families nurture who they are, their identity. But out in the world, it doesn't. And it's sad because a lot of times they get lost and they get confused. They don't know who they are anymore, because they

end up coming home. They can't succeed out there. But it's because they don't have that support system. They're going to struggle. They really will struggle because they don't have that support system. And they're used to having support. They're used to having family.

## People Who Are Survivors

"They're used to having family." In many respects this statement summarizes the tribal strengths associated with having a strong tribal identity for American Indian youth. *Tiyospaye* is the Lakota word for family, and its meaning includes deeply textured nuances.[6] Tiyospaye is more than one's immediate and extended family members. Its meaning includes a place of dwelling, sense of belonging, and deep-rooted connection. It includes obligations, responsibilities, morality, and spirituality in relation to others as well as to oneself. Among the Siouan peoples, tiyospaye locates a person's sense of self in a web of relationships that is greater than the individual person, and virtually all other tribal nations hold similar notions (Lakota Dakota Nakota Language Preservation Summit, 2014).

Tribal identity does not develop in a social vacuum, and it only has meaning within a cultural-historical context. It is at once and the same time a personal expression and a collective possession. As the Montana middle schooler so aptly put it, "I belong to a unique set of people who are survivors! We are still here. I love being Native!"

If all these things are true about tribal identity, then they beg the question, how do Native educators practice their craft in such ways to build the tribal strengths, including tribal identity, among American Indian students? Just as important, what obstructions stand in the way of Native educators cultivating those strengths? To these questions, the six American Indian educators had much to say.

# 4

## Tribal Strengths and the Craft of Teaching

One of our goals is to learn more about the culture and how to be culturally proficient. So that's what we're working on . . . Our students, they need to be able to say "I am a Lakota."

—LORI, South Dakota educator

The late Chief Dan George was largely known to the public as an actor turning in a number of memorable performances opposite some of Hollywood's leading celebrities.[1] But among other achievements in George's long and fascinating life, he was also an accomplished poet. In his celebrated collection of poems *My Heart Soars,* George included an untitled stanza followed by an untitled one-line poem. Taken together they read:

> Of all the teachings we receive
> this one is the most important:
> Nothing belongs to you
> of what there is,
> of what you take,
> you must share.
> Touch a child—they are my people.

George's richly beautiful words serve as a reminder of the enduring responsibility adults have toward their most precious cultural resource. It also acknowledges the powerful affect personal interaction will have on a child. Adult-child relationships have an impact that lasts for a lifetime. Educators bear a special obligation in realizing the full implications of this simple truism. Yet I find it disconcerting the number of American

Indian educators who have told me about negative experiences attending schools while they were students. The stories take the same general pattern, more or less. They involve an insensitive non-Native teacher who openly espoused racially stereotypical sentiments designed to demean American Indians. The teacher remained indifferent to the embarrassed and hurt feelings of the Native student. Sometimes the narrative includes a blatant racist verbal attack directed personally at the student. The result is the demoralization of the individual who was left dealing with self-doubt and feelings of inferiority that took years to overcome. Ultimately, the person made a deliberate choice to reverse the damage inflicted. That choice, ironically enough, included the decision to become an educator himself/herself. The particulars of the story may vary slightly, but the motivation is always the same. The choice to become an educator allowed the person to serve Native children in a culturally and emotionally healthy manner.

It happened to Tammy.[2] She freely described her difficult high school years dealing with several teachers, individuals who, by any fair assessment, were nothing less than racists. There is no reason to be polite about it. Tammy's description (which I believe if anything undersold the drama involved) convinces me that a few of her former teachers held deeply disturbing, racist beliefs about American Indian peoples. And she grasped all too well the potential consequences of these types of experiences. At our last meeting, I once again asked Tammy about her early encounters with racism in the classroom. She reflected, "These were teachers that were there for years and years and years and years. How many kids did they chase off from the high school? They had a high percentage of dropouts at that time. If I wasn't strong and if I didn't have strong parents that helped me, that raised me to have opinions, I would just probably be in the background too and think that way."

Tammy raised a fair, albeit troubling, question. Over the decades, how many students were chased away from school by the very individuals charged with their education? I am not suggesting in any way that most non-Native educators are racists and do little but inflict emotional harm on Native students. I personally know far too many dedicated, caring, and, yes, culturally sensitive non-Native educators serving in reservation schools to make such an outrageous and unfair assertion. Conversely, there are also some incompetent, uncaring, culturally indifferent Native educators in reservation schools who probably should not be anywhere near a classroom. But even acknowledging these facts, it remains that there is something special and highly significant about passionate, competent American Indian educators teaching American Indian children—they touch a child because they are their people.

## Perspectives from Scholars

Anyone doing research on the best teaching practices for American Indian students will not be disappointed by an absence of treatment in the scholarly literature. Likely only investigations on factors associated with academic achievement eclipse discussions on the actual practice of teaching American Indians. Two themes in particular stand out. First, scholars and practitioners debate what constitutes effective education for Native students. Especially prominent are debates on appropriate pedagogy and curriculum. Second, they have identified a number of important controversies connected to American Indian education. Notable among these controversies are concerns over the misunderstanding and misuse of Native cultures and histories and stereotyping of American Indian students.

### AMERICAN INDIAN EDUCATORS AND THE EFFECTIVE EDUCATION OF NATIVE STUDENTS

First Nations educator Anita Keith put the matter bluntly: "Most Euro-Canadians historically did not have sensitivity to Native culture, nor did they understand how the Native education is inherently and structurally different" (2004, p. 7). One would have to assume that Keith would likely include Euro-Americans in her conclusion as well. Yet, Keith also suggests that this historical shortcoming need not continue. All educators, both Native and non-Native, can effectively teach Native students. She argues, "There is a need to affirm the qualities that permeate Native life: respect for family, the preciousness of children and youth, honouring Elders, pride in tribal craftsmanship, listening to one's neighbor, being discreet (especially when another's honour and dignity are concerned), taking time to be introspective and contemplative about the mysteries of the universe, and valuing oral traditions that engender humbleness, sharing, and laughter" (p. 8). In essence, Keith insists that deeper understanding and appreciation for shared values common among Native peoples will produce long-range educational benefits. Nevertheless, her observations point to a complex issue, namely, what constitutes the most effective education for Native students?

One of the sharpest debates currently in education circles involves the nature of culturally relevant education. There are no shortage of opinions on this topic either.[3] Be that as it may, the issue of culturally relevant education for Native students is more than just another passing educational fad or, worse, a hollow exercise in political correctness[4] (Klug & Whitfield, 2003; Swisher & Tippeconnic, 1999). Given the alarmingly high rates of educational attrition common among Native students at the secondary and postsecondary levels, it should be clear that past educational practices are not working as they should. Thus, culturally relevant education takes on an importance and perhaps even an urgency for students, parents, and educators. Generally, culturally relevant education is thought to consist of two parts. On the one hand, it needs to be grounded on culturally sensitive teaching practices. On the other, it must also include culturally appropriate curriculum. In other words, culturally relevant education includes how teachers teach (pedagogy) and what they teach (curriculum).

Roland Tharp argues, "The crucial element of the classroom is pedagogy. Pedagogy here refers to the organization of instructional activity and the patterns of teacher and student relationship. In classrooms for Native Americans, students will achieve and prosper to the degree that the appropriate pedagogy is practiced" (2006, p. 6). But what constitutes "appropriate pedagogy"? The answer may not be as perplexing as it appears. Scholars and practitioners agree that culturally sensitive teaching practices must build on the cultural strengths of Native students (Cleary & Peacock, 1998; Lomawaima & McCarty, 2006; Swisher & Tippeconnic, 1999; Van Hamme, 1996). Moreover, some have articulated the specific, unique cultural strengths possessed by American Indian students and outlined necessary modifications in teaching practices that can effectively use them. For instance, teaching practices can utilize methods congruent with communication styles and preferences common in the local tribal community; integrate tribal values and worldview in lesson plans; engage in deliberate examinations of historical contributions of Native tribes and individuals; examine contemporary issues important to tribal communities; incorporate student's tribal language and concepts into classroom and school-wide programs; and encourage tribal members and elders to participate in the education of Native students (Barnhardt & Kawagley, 2005; Cleary & Peacock, 1998; Cummings, 1992; Huffman, 2010; Klug & Whitfield, 2003; Lomawaima & McCarty, 2006; Yazzie, 1999). Indeed, a growing number of studies report successful results when educators deliberately strive to utilize and build on existing cultural strengths of Native students (see, for instance, Cheeseman & Gapp, 2012; Inglebret, Jones, & CHiXapkaid, 2008; McCarty, 2002; McCarty, Wallace, Lynch, & Benally, 1991; Nam, Roehrig, Kern, & Reynolds, 2012).

Culturally appropriate curriculum presents more troublesome issues than culturally sensitive pedagogy and invites a number of significant questions (Yazzie-Mintz, 2007). Namely, curriculum that is culturally appropriate for whom? Who is qualified to develop such curriculum? Perhaps most critical of all, will all the necessary stakeholders (including policymakers, tribal leaders, educators, and parents) be desirous to commit to the funding, planning, and resource allocation necessary to develop sweeping American Indian culturally appropriate curriculum? Obviously, these questions are interconnected and represent significant challenges for the many stakeholders involved.

The question about curriculum that is culturally appropriate is potentially a politically charged issue. Culturally appropriate curriculum may take three forms. First, curriculum may be presented as shared history and perspectives common among Native peoples, a kind of generic approach to Native education (Pewewardy, 1998a, 1999). This is essentially the approach of Montana's Indian Education for All initiative, which attempts to introduce and integrate the history and values of the state's various tribal nations across the school curriculum[5] (Kelting-Gibson, 2006). Second, curriculum may be presented in a tribally specific fashion in which the language, history, and customs of a tribal nation are emphasized (Hermes, 2007; Tippeconnic & Tippeconnic Fox, 2012; Lomawaima, 1995). These attempts have been demonstrated to be highly effective. However, difficulties can arise for reservation communities populated by more than one tribal nation. Potential controversies over which nation's language, history, and customs is perceived to be given greater or lesser emphasis can plague and frustrate educators' efforts to deliver what they desire to be culturally appropriate curriculum (Littlebear, 1999; Ngai, 2008). Third, educators can combine elements of both a shared history and tribal-specific curriculum. Researchers have also reported general success with this approach, although even these efforts can run into the problems related to intertribal differences, tensions, and preferences (Mihesuah, 2003; Sparks, 2000).

The issue also arises of who will develop the curriculum considered to be culturally appropriate. The obvious answer would be American Indian educators working in conjunction with tribal elders (Cleary & Peacock, 1998; Lipka, Sharp, Brenner, Yanez, & Sharp, 2005; Lomawaima & McCarty, 2006; Swisher & Tippeconnic, 1999). However, as it currently stands, there are few American Indian educators serving in the nation's classrooms (Erikson et al., 2008; Huffman, 2013). Moreover, there are likely even fewer who have the desire and ability to produce effective materials. Yet, this challenge is hardly insurmountable and should not be considered a prohibitive barrier. They may be few in number, yet professionally motivated and culturally qualified individuals do exist. With time and determined efforts, their numbers are sure to grow (Huffman, 2013). Nevertheless, time is a critical factor as many elders, the crucial keepers of tribal wisdom and culture, are aging, and their numbers are dwindling quickly.

The commitment necessary to realize culturally appropriate curriculum poses special challenges. It is one thing to offer rhetoric encouraging such curriculum innovations; it is quite another to fund and allocate the resources necessary for those efforts (Bell & Marlow, 2009). As Donna Martinez points out, "While some states have passed legislation to support teaching about American Indians, no funding to support culturally relevant curriculum changes or teacher training accompany these measures" (2014, p. 202). But this commitment requires more than just funding. It also includes a willingness to examine the nature of curriculum and even the way students' academic progress is assessed (Fenimore-Smith, 2009; Huffman, 2013; Martinez, 2014). This ultimately will require a complete reexamination of the educational system for American Indian children (perhaps all American children) (Forbes, 2000). One has to question whether the political will is present for such drastic evaluation and reform.

That last point connects to yet another hot-topic political

issue—student assessment and curricular requirements. The debate over culturally appropriate curriculum has become especially sharp as a result of the standards-based initiatives driving educational policy over the last few decades. The policy of No Child Left Behind (NCLB) ushered in the era of school accountability (Ravitch, 2010). Under NCLB, school districts, schools, and educators were subjected to sanctions for chronically low scores in the subject areas of reading and mathematics.[6] As a result, a growing concern surrounds an alleged narrowing of the curriculum in which educators concentrate on such "high stakes" subjects as reading and mathematics (which are subject to standardized assessment testing) at the expense of "low stakes" subjects such as history, social studies, or literature (which are not subject to standardized assessment testing) (Jones, Jones, & Hargrove, 2003; Ravitch, 2010). Subsequently, tribal cultural education efforts such as tribal language and history courses have been squeezed out by the time and effort needed to concentrate on acquiring higher scores in the standardized reading and math assessments[7] (Huffman, 2013; McCarty, 2008; Winstead et al., 2008).

Ultimately, the effective education of Native students depends in great measure on the culturally qualified, professionally trained educators working closely with tribal elders and other stakeholders to craft the appropriate practices and fashion the curriculum. A tall order to be sure, but already there is proof that such measures are not only possible but can work effectively. Referring to the efforts of Navajo educators to develop and implement culturally appropriate instruction methods and curriculum, Tarajean Yazzie-Mintz relates, "There is great wisdom, power, and authority that Navajo teachers contribute to the study of culturally appropriate curriculum and pedagogy. Their experiences and words provide key insights into the multiple ways in which this approach to teaching can be implemented in classrooms serving Navajo students. Moreover, the documentation of existing knowledge and reflective practice in Indian education provides a window through which educators of American Indian students can participate, reflect, and develop culturally relevant modes of teaching and learning" (2007, p. 73).

CONTROVERSIES IN AMERICAN INDIAN EDUCATION

Walter Fleming, professor of Native American Studies at Montana State University and author of *The Complete Idiot's Guide to Native American*

*History*, has suggested, "When it comes to Americans' knowledge about Native American culture and history, one might say there are two types of people—those who know nothing about Natives and those who know less than that" (2006, p. 213). Humorous overstatement though it may be, it is hard to argue with Fleming's assertion that many people possess little understanding of their fellow Native American citizens. Likely for good reasons Fleming contends, "Because many people have such a limited knowledge of Indians, we are, arguably, among the most misunderstood ethnic groups in the United States" (p. 213). Unfortunately, this general lack of understanding extends to educators. As one non-Native teacher in Montana admitted, "A year ago I knew very little about American Indian history, and what I did know about Montana's tribes could have been gleaned from a tourism brochure. That's because I—like most other Americans—am a product of a system of education that simply does not include Indians" (Warren, 2006, p. 198).

An especially important issue for American Indian education scholars and practitioners is the ongoing discussion about the misunderstanding and misuse of tribal histories, identities, and intellectual/spiritual property in educational settings. Most notable is the concern regarding the teaching of American Indian history and culture. It is an incredibly complex issue touching on powerful notions of sovereignty rights over identity, freedom of expression, respect for tribal spirituality, and much more (Wilson, 2004). Michael Kent Ward warns against the potential for misunderstanding of Native history, traditions, and customs by individuals who are unqualified to present authentic narratives. According to Ward the risk is that "old stereotypes and biases become replaced with new ones" (2011, p. 106). He argues:

> As part of the social science curriculum, the study and academic interpretations of American Indian culture and history regularly attracts educators and students alike, but remains problematic for reasons of cultural property and identity. Of particular concern are matters related to the accuracy and purposes of such instructional content and problems of cultural representation, cultural boundaries and cultural and/or intellectual property . . . Another problem has to do with cultural property and the use of cultural items—both tangible and intangible—by non-Indians and Native Americans alike, who lack the support of traditional Indians and indigenous authorities for such uses (Brown, 1998). An associated feature of this issue has to do with the idea that such items taken outside

their cultural contexts lose their efficacy and meaning and therefore should not be used. In the end, the main problem again, is one of identity as Native Americans realize the undermining of their authority and the theft of their culture by persons who freely claim the right to re-imagine indigenous peoples according to their definitions. (pp. 104, 106)

Further, Ward describes the particularly egregious misuse of Native spiritual expressions among educators (among others). This issue is an especially powerful one that is understandably concerning to tribal nations. Ward asserts, "It is often the case that expressions of indigenous spirituality accompany many standard interpretations of American Indians. For example, simplified versions of Native American purification ceremonies, sacred histories or myths, songs, dances, and other cultural elements are frequently included in presentations about indigenous cultures, without correct or adequate interpretation related to the deep meaning attached to them, or sans appropriate contexts for their use" (2011, p. 109).

The misuse of American Indian spirituality can and, in fact, does find its way into American classrooms. As Cornel Pewewardy warns,

> Be very cautious when teaching children about song and dance. Singing or dancing "Indian style" and "having a pow-wow" to many children today, is "cool." On the other hand, many traditional people do not see their tribal culture as cool. It is traditional and should be treated with respect and honor. Children should not dance Hollywood Indian-style, nor should children beat on a drum and try to sing traditional songs. Social and traditional songs and dances have religious meaning for many tribes and any attempt at imitation is ridicule. The ability to beat on the drum and sing song is earned through tribal rites of passage. (1998b, p. 72)

These classroom practices may seem rather benign to some. But activities such as those described by Pewewardy and Ward involve the basic human right to one's own cultural identity as well as the integrity of spiritual expression. Pewewardy declares, "Today, I see silent genocide in the way indigenous people are integrated and reinvented by non-Indians. Appropriation of indigenous ceremonies, religions, and identities has been the most threatening practice" (1998b, p. 73). Educators bear a special responsibility to respectfully listen and heed such impassioned assertions made by tribal elders, Native scholars, and tribal members.

Certainly related to the misuse of and misunderstanding of tribal cultures and histories is concern over the superficial, if not trivial, treatment of Native peoples in curricular materials or pedagogical presentations. Just as a lack of true understanding or active misuse of tribal histories and culture is damaging, so too are superficial representations of American Indian peoples. Part of the apprehension is that tribal images and artifacts that are merely convenient to the teacher may be presented in the classroom in an attempt to "teach about Indians." These opportune pedagogical methods, however, are in reality shallow and unrealistic treatments that potentially can do more harm than good. Ellen Swaney, former director of American Indian / Minority Achievement in Montana's Office of the Commissioner of Higher Education makes this compelling argument:

> My concern is that instruction might end up trivializing highly complex cultural issues. For example, Indian culture is often presented through the arts, especially our traditional arts such as powwows, dancing, and beadwork. These visual representations are often the best known and most easily demonstrated aspects of a culture, but they are not *the* culture. Rather, they are a manifestation of a much broader and more complex set of value orientations. To present such a narrow cross section of a culture trivializes the richness and complexity of the lives of Native peoples. It does not begin to touch upon how our Native beliefs, attitudes, and values, verbal and nonverbal language and objects and artifacts affect our views of authority, relationships, action, and time. Our views tend to be on the opposite end of the spectrum from the values of mainstream American culture, and unfamiliarity sometimes breeds contempt. Educators and students must understand that, while Native perceptions of the world may be different, they are not deficient . . . Moreover, really exploring culture raises thorny issues about the culture of the American school system. Honestly engaging IEFA [Indian Education for All, the Montana State initiative] requires us to consider the political, economic, and power issues involved with including people who are culturally different. Such discussions will be difficult, but anything less will result in superficial treatment of a fundamentally important component of this law. (2006, pp. 190–91)

Deirdre Almeida (1996) argues that inadequate teacher training, lingering stereotypical portrayals of American Indians, and the lack of culturally trustworthy pedagogical materials exacerbate the superficial treatment of Native cultures and histories. But Almeida also suggests another common concern found in the literature, namely, the treatment

of American Indian students based on preconceived notions and stereotypical images by non-Native educators and by scholars. This issue takes
a number of forms in the literature, from the contentious notion that
Native students lack a motivation to achieve (Aragon, 2002; Bryde, 1971)
to the tendency to regard American Indian students as possessing specific
and frequently stereotypical learning styles (Guild, 1994; Pewewardy,
2002). While recognizing the cultural differences in learning, Hani Morgan warns against overgeneralizations of Native students. She suggests,
"Although it is dangerous to overgeneralize, research has shown that
Native American students are likely to behave and react to teachers and
teaching strategies in specific ways that are often different from mainstream students. In order to avoid stereotyping and overgeneralizing,
teachers should observe students before assuming they will respond in
certain ways that reflect anticipated cultural learning styles" (2009, p. 11).

Some educators may also operate on the faulty assumption that
Native students are culturally and socially disadvantaged. Consciously
or unconsciously, they may treat American Indian students in a conde-
scending manner, perhaps even hold lower academic expectations for
them (Morgan, 2009; Strong, 1998). Ironically, these educators may also
run the risk of being blinded to their own cultural deficits. Pewewardy
points out, "Many teachers speak of American Indian students as being
disadvantaged. In reality, many Indian students have the double advantage of knowing and living in several cultures. The teacher, on the other
hand, may know only one culture and may have accepted that culture as
being superior without any real thought or study. It is the teacher, then,
who is disadvantaged" (1998b, p. 74).

## Voices from the Reservation Classroom

The six individuals included in this study are careful, diligent educators.
They all have a sustained record of dedicated service. Their perspectives
on the craft of teaching in reservation classrooms offer a great deal of
wisdom. Our conversations exposed two prevailing themes regarding
teaching in reservation classrooms. Moreover, these themes generally
reflect the issues found in the scholarly literature. The educators discussed a variety of approaches and practices they employ to effectively
teach American Indian children. Essentially, these include their ideas on

culturally relevant teaching practices and ways to infuse tribal culture into their classrooms. But they did not stop there. They also frankly discussed important barriers that work against fully taking advantage of tribal strengths in the education of reservation children.

### TEACHING PRACTICES AND TRIBAL STRENGTHS

The educators spoke of both formal and informal ways they attempt to infuse tribal strengths into their practice. Most such efforts seem rather spontaneous. And in many respects they are; however, there is also a deliberate strategy at work. Their narratives indicate that they look for and are prepared for "teachable moments." These spur-of-the-moment episodes may not be clearly outlined in a formal lesson plan, but the educators anticipate them and are prepared to take advantage when they occur. For instance, Tammy related, "How I feel about things is that you prove it by your actions. So, if I say I am Native American, I should have respect for my elders. I should share. I should not be prideful of what I have. You know, that is just how we were brought up. That is what I tell my kids and that's what we do in the class."

They understood that informal and spontaneous efforts have a tremendous impact on the value formation and identity development of children. The participants described working to build on the tribal strengths of their people in ways to which their students can relate and from which they can ultimately benefit. Justin reflected deeply about his pedagogical philosophy as a Native educator serving Native students. It was clear he had given this issue a great deal of thought long before we had engaged in our conversations. He discussed at length how he attempts to guide students' attitudes on what it means to be an American Indian in today's society. For example, he described his attempts to guide his students into critical thinking about how current ceremonial practices have been altered and removed from their traditional values and meaning.

> When there's a giveaway up here now, they give away to the politicians and all the people who have influence. But what actually happened in a traditional giveaway is that you found the people who were the poorest and you gave them as much as you could. Maybe some people have giveaways like that; but when you go to the cultural events here today you don't see that. At the Sun Dances and powwows people give their

things to the people who already have the most. That's not part of the values! The redistribution of wealth, that's been lost. I try to get my kids to see it the best they can . . . There's opportunities for it and I think I've kind of not taken advantage of the opportunities that I could have had sometimes. But I'm trying, and the kids are being exposed to those values. And also thinking about what's behind that value. We talk about cooperation; talk about everybody helping each other out and lifting each other up. We're not competing against each other; we have to make each other better. That's another traditional value—where you take care of each other. You lift each other up; you help each other out. Then in turn those people will help you out, and everybody makes everybody else's life a little bit better and a little bit easier. We try to practice that right here in the classroom as best we can.

Rachel described a teachable moment that occurred just days before I came for a visit to her school. In this instance the students were curious to know why they had to stand and be quiet each morning during the Lakota Flag Song which initiates each day for their school.[8] Rachel took the time to discuss not only the importance and meaning of the Flag Song but also the practice of smudging, which too is a daily ritual in her second grade class.[9] It is a remarkable account of how a teacher who is well versed in the tribal legacy of her nation and possessing a well-defined tribal identity can guide young Native children into a greater understanding of their tribal strengths.

I said, "We do this because we're honoring the people that died for us. A lot of our people went to war to fight for our country so that we remained free." And I said, "And so, when we have the Flag Song, I ask you guys to be quiet out of respect." And I said, "Our people based a lot on respect. So, you guys need to be respectful and stand and let the Flag Song finish without talking and visiting and stuff. There's just that few minutes that have to be there. Let's be quiet and that's showing the respect." I said, "Remember that. We always talk to you guys about respect, but that's part of who we are as a people." And then, we were smudging, and that's another part that the kids initiated themselves—my second-graders! I think they did it last year a lot, in [name of first grade teacher] room, and they'll do it a lot in [name of third grade teacher] room. And they said, "Can we smudge, teacher?" and I said, "Yes. We can. I'm glad you brought that up." And I said, "The only thing—the only reason I haven't done it before is because I forgot my shell and my fan at home." Well, now, we got my fan and the shell, and I just bring a hawk fan, you know, to smudge here; I don't bring my eagle fan. And so they will smudge themselves, and they'll ask questions like, "Why do we smudge?" "What is this called?" "What is it in Lakota?" I'll say, "Okay, what do you call it in Lakota?" And they'll know! And I'll say, "So, why do we burn the sage? Why are we burning this?" "Because it smells good!" they say. And I say, "Mm-hmm." As soon as I smell that, it has that automatic calming to me. I say, "So, and what else? Why else do we burn it?" And they say, "So that we chase all the bad spirits away." I say, "Yes, that's right. Any time we get ready for any ceremonies, people will smudge us, because we're chasing the spirits away." So then I ask, "Why do we burn the sweet grass? What does that do?" And there's a young man in there that I know is real, real tradition, and he'll answer. He'll say, "That's to bring the good spirits in." "Yes," I say, "when we burn the sweet grass that calls all the good spirits. We want them to come there when we're having the ceremony." So, I say, "You're right. Now, we're smudging ourselves; we are getting ready; we're cleansing ourselves; we're getting ready for the day. You guys don't know it, but every morning, on the way to work, I pray." And I say, "One of the things I pray for is for you: your spirit—that the spirit will watch over you and get you ready and keep you prepared and get your mind alert and ready for the day for learning."

Donna also regarded the Flag Song and smudging as important in shaping the tribal identities of the students at her elementary school. She, however, expressed concern because the young students frequently have their tribal identities challenged when they move into middle school. The middle school, it should be noted, is located in a less traditional community and serves children from a variety of reservation communities. As Donna viewed it, the educators at the middle school were not consistent in reinforcing tribal identities and utilizing tribal practices. "We start today with the Flag Song and some of the teachers smudge in the classroom. They [the students] lose that when they go to middle school. The middle school is doing a better job of transitioning. They bring the students in and they make it a weeklong thing to transition in and it's getting better. But it's a hard transition for these students to do."

The educators outlined specific practices besides informal and spontaneous episodes designed to build the tribal strengths of students. They discussed deliberate, concentrated attempts to create or find curricular materials that can be used to support their personal pedagogical efforts. For instance, Tammy told of a favorite class activity among her students. It should be noted that Tammy, a math teacher, introduced this activity to her students.

You know what they really, really like? They like Native stories! Let me show you the book I was reading to them! It's a Lakota book. And it has Lakota stories. They really like the one about the man who—they were hunting antelope and—I wonder if somebody took it! [Laughs] The hunters were chasing antelope and one hunter could outrun the antelope. It's a generational story; they like stories like that. You know? So I'll read it to them and they'll say, "Get in those [inaudible]." Oral history, it's true! [Laughs] You never know until you try. [Laughs] You know? But I'll say, "What was the thing he did first? He prayed. He prayed—asked the Creator to help him catch this antelope because they were starving." So just that makes a difference.

I could almost feel the pride forming among the students during Tammy's enthusiastic recounting of their reaction to the antelope story. Donna related, "We have teachers that are fluent in the language and they speak it in their classrooms. And some of the aides are fluent. That's not anywhere else. And in the literacy cultures, the teachers want to come into these teachers' classrooms just to sit in and see how and what they're doing."

Justin was perhaps the most idealistic of the six participants. He carefully and consistently described his desire to see a radical reform in the curriculum used in reservation schools. For him, culturally appropriate curriculum needs to be deliberately created around prominent tribal values. He suggested,

I believe that as opposed to a standards-based curriculum an Indian community needs a values-based curriculum. Then you can bring in your standards underneath that. But you have to teach values first. It's kind of a different way of seeing the world. Like old ways of looking at things where you put the people first. It's not the individual; it's not the family; it's the people. If the people are doing well then the families will be doing well. Then the individuals will be doing well. But if everybody's just out for themselves, that's not the traditional value. That's an American cultural value; individual freedom; the strength of the nuclear family. Whereas ours is the extended family. Teaching kids to be respectful. I think that's a word we throw around a lot, especially in our school. But our kids aren't always respectful. But to be respectful is a cultural strength.

Justin's vision for a value-based curriculum aligns with the direction taken in Lori's South Dakota school district. She described systematic and systemic efforts to introduce the tribal legacy (including history, language, and, most notable, traditional values) of the Lakota people into the district's curriculum. The objectives of her school district sound much like the desired direction articulated by Justin. Lori reflected,

> Our district has developed a curriculum called "Living the Lakota Way." It's taking our virtues, the values of our tribe that we believe in and that make you a good person. It's a cultural-based character model. So we're using that district-wide in our schools, and we're hoping that our kids will realize that I am Native American. I see these virtues still being lived on the reservation, and we want try to get our students to start living them because they're out there. We have so much gang activity going on right now. And one of the other things that we're doing in the district is reading the book *Teaching with Poverty in Mind.* I think for a long time people thought that what they see out in the community is a breakdown of the culture. But that is what happens when poverty is involved along with the trauma of the boarding school era. There are so many complex things involved that our students don't know who they are anymore as Native Americans. So we're taking that move now to start bringing cultural virtues back. That way they will have that pride. Because right now they're not succeeding in school academically because of that. That's one of the reasons why they're not. We're hoping that by doing some of these things that we won't see so many of these kids getting off the bus and heading the opposite way of the school. And we've done surveys. We've surveyed the students and asked what is it that we need to do as educators? And they say school is boring. So one of the things that we're trying to do is to bring more of the culture into the classroom so they can be engaged and to introduce teaching strategies that work better with Native American students. We know that our kids like to work in a group, so we're doing some of those types of strategies with them to see if that will make a difference. Some of our schools are teaching the language at the middle school. The high school is doing that too. Taking one step at a time. So we'll see what happens. But at least it's not the old pullout or having Title XII programs hire Native Americans to go into the classroom for a half hour and teach. It's that we have to embed this in our classrooms all the time. As administrators it's our responsibility to bring that awareness to the staff and teach them about the culture so that they can teach it in the classroom.

## BARRIERS TO TRIBAL STRENGTHS IN SCHOOLS

While the six educators were generally optimistic about the prospects of infusing tribal strengths into the classroom, they also recognized significant barriers to these efforts. It is revealing that all six admitted that they did not feel they were personally doing enough to utilize their tribal legacy in the classroom. Even given her obvious enthusiasm, Tammy confessed, "I think I don't do enough either. I mean, I don't think anybody can. We just have to do what we can, when we can. I don't know what else we can do more." Justin discussed his desire to increase his efforts to infuse tribal cultural history and traditions in his teaching practice. Yet he acknowledged feelings of falling short.

> I'm still trying to figure it out. I'm here doing what I can, and I'm starting to realize it's not enough. What I'm doing is not enough. I love it and I'm happy with what I do, but I feel like I've got to do more based on what I want to see happen . . . You got to shoot for ideas. You got to shoot for things the best way that you think they should be. You got to work towards it, and when things aren't like what you know needs to happen it's tough to see it. It's tough to see these kids and what challenges they have; what they don't have. You know they go home and some of them don't have enough food; some of them don't have anybody teaching them; some of them don't have anybody to talk to. But it's got to start somewhere. I think school is a place where the culture was taken away from them. So I think school is a place where it can be brought back. Teach these kids the culture and change a generation. I believe that. But we've got to figure out how to do it, how to implement it. Indian Education for All is a good idea, but we've got to find a way to figure out what that means. Does it mean dressing up as Indians at Thanksgiving, or Columbus Day, or something deeper than all that?

Five of the educators identified superficial efforts to infuse tribal strengths in pedagogy and curriculum as a barrier to the effective education of American Indian students. Regarding some of the shallow attempts in her school district, Lori observed, "I've said to all the administrators, 'When you walk into your schools, there's nothing that shows who they are as a culture, as a tribe, even something as simple as that.' Some schools are now starting to smudge in the morning. They're bringing the drum groups in. But for some schools it would be like if you were walking into a school in Sioux Falls. It was all the cutesy little things on the wall and stuff. But there is nothing that really said we have Native American students in this building!"

While acknowledging his school district's efforts at building tribally relevant pedagogy and curriculum, Ben was nevertheless frustrated by the lack of cultural depth. He desired to see wider and deeper cultural meanings introduced to the students on his reservation. He declared, "What we do in school is we put a huge emphasis on incorporating local culture into the curriculum. And we see a lot of it when we visit classrooms, which is good. But it's still only at that surface level. If I was in charge of the whole thing, in charge of education for our school and could do anything, I would like to mandate more in depth. Let's build a sweat lodge on the grounds. Let's do those things, and let's tell kids, 'This is where you come from.' I don't think it'll ever happen. It's too controversial, and you can get yourself in hot water. But I think it's a big part of the solution."

Ben's remarks reveal another apprehension voiced by all six educators, namely, that integration of tribal values, worldviews, history, and especially spirituality (which they all regard as an absolutely essential tribal strength) will potentially invite controversy. Their concern especially centered on the infusion of tribal spirituality in the classroom and how some people would regard this as a violation of the separation of church and state. All the educators work on reservations, yet all the schools receive government funding. In other words, they all work in schools operating with a memo of understanding (MOU) with their respective state to operate the school district. Thus, their concerns over potential controversy are not necessarily misplaced.

These educators come from profoundly spiritual tribes.[10] They all agreed that any discussion on tribal strengths must necessarily include tribal spirituality. The spirituality of their people is central to and intertwined with all aspects of their respective cultures. In essence, to speak of tribal strengths requires them to include tribal notions of spirituality. Donna explained, "I can see that [controversy over spirituality] for teachers who do not know our culture. We know the difference in spirituality and religion. I mean, I'm a Catholic, but I still do the Lakota ways. But I mean they don't understand there is a difference. We've had teachers that come in and because we do the Flag Song in the morning and some classrooms smudge, they think we're pushing a religion on them. They can't understand that. But everything we do is spirituality because it is part of who we are as Lakota people." Lori voiced views similar to Donna. For Lori, the spirituality of the Lakota people is not the same as an organized religion. Rather, it is an integral and inherent aspect of simply being Lakota. To require a Lakota person to refrain from expressing his/her spirituality is to ask that individual to stop being Lakota. She put the matter this way, "We used to have that fear when we first started doing that [starting the school day with the Flag Song and smudging]. You know, the separation of state. But because we look at it differently, this isn't a religion. I mean, Lakota people do have, that is, some people do practice the traditional Lakota religion, but that's something separate. Being spiritual is just how you live. So that's in here [points to her heart]. It's right here. And that's how we've always argued. Because we've had school board members that said, 'You need to take this out.' It was when the superintendent, our previous superintendent, came on they asked for community members to help them write the vision and statement of belief."

Nevertheless, the participants were sensitive to the possible protestations from non-Natives (and other Natives for that matter) who may object to what they may see as unfair considerations given to reservation schools. Tammy spoke directly to this issue. "I think as a school, the separation of church and state is an issue. We all need something—a higher being, a Creator—whatever you think to be accountable to. Some of these kids don't have nothing or nobody, and they need that. They need to have something to pray to, and we talk about that sort of thing." Likewise, Ben understood the potential for controversy and religious offense. With complete frankness he said, "If you want to talk about and truly expose kids to what a sweat lodge is, there's no way in the world you're going do it without offending someone who's doesn't live or lead that lifestyle or, more important, someone who is not a traditionalist, someone who's a Christian. You're going to offend someone because you cannot teach about that sweat lodge without teaching about why it's there and touching the religious, spiritual brace of it. And you will offend someone."

Lori described her tribe's reservation-wide efforts designed to revitalize Lakota language and culture. She was adamant that these efforts required the support and cooperation of everyone and needed all the resources the tribe could muster. Yet, she related that some of the strongest support came from young, new-to-the-profession, non-Native teachers. Ironically, some of the strongest opposition came from a few Native educators. Her remarks suggest the complexity of working toward the most culturally effective education for American Indian students. Lori offered this astute observation:

One thing that we've been finding which has been interesting, as we talk to the teachers and we talk to the administrators and we talk more about poverty and the culture, the non-Natives who are coming to our reservations are so willing to learn and just wanting to know what it is they need to do to help reach our students. The people that are resisting it the most are the people—the local Native American teachers, and so we had a discussion about it at our last admin meeting . . . I've said this before, if we, if the tribe feels that the language is so important and the culture is so important then they have to start doing something; then we need to build partnerships and grab all the resources that we have; all the speakers that we have; and start taking some action. That's where I thought we were going last year when we were having all these meetings. And as we sat around the table we agreed that, yeah, well, maybe we do need to get into the communities. We have technology; we have better resources; we can go to a site and bring families in. And our tribal president, I think, is on the same path of thinking that we've got to do something. We can't rely on the schools to be doing this all the time. I keep thinking what happened? So, we have a long way to go to fix this problem. But I think we're on the right track by going into the community. There's a day care here on the reservation where they are speaking the language to these babies. That's all they speak. So now Head Start is realizing that we're going to have to learn. Then the schools will have to get involved or the communities will have to get involved to keep this going and growing. But it's going to take a lot of effort. Kids need to know why their culture is so important. And there are things that are happening. There's camps, summer camps, that the tribe has. And, so, there are efforts being made, but it's going to take a long time. I mean, it took years for this to happen, our cultural loss, and it's going to take years to undo it.

## The Give and Take of Teaching

Teaching gives to and it takes from a person. It gives a person a sense of meaning and purpose. Yet, the routine of teaching can drain the energy from the most passionate of educators. Given the demands placed on teachers, it should not come as a surprise that this book, consistent with previous research, reveals a vulnerability of sorts among American Indian educators. Frequently, Native educators reflect that they need to do more for their people. They need to contribute more toward the preservation of tribal cultures (Beynon, 2008; Kitchen et al., 2009); they need to do more to protect and educate Native youth (Cherubini et al., 2010).

I appreciate the humility of the individuals who participated in this investigation. I also respect their personal sense of responsibility. But I also point out something very important. The good work of individual educators is crucial, but as individuals they operate within the context of an institution. Reservation schools shoulder major responsibility to provide the culture, the resources, and the leadership that allow teachers to "do more." Institutionally and systemically, reservation schools ultimately serve or fail to serve Native American children.

Rachel stressed that the integration of tribal strengths must enjoy both full community and full institutional support. For her, the effective teaching of Native children requires a clarion call to action. She passionately asserted, "If this community takes a collectiveness, it's like tapping into that collectiveness. We want our kids to learn this. And we have to have the teachers buy into that; we have to have the community buy into that. We're going to do this; we can do this! We're going to teach our kids to have the generosity, to have the fortitude, to have the bravery in order to go on through life."

# 5

# Tribal Strengths and Reservation Schools

> I think school is a place where the culture was taken away from them. So I think school is a place where it can be brought back. Teach these kids the culture and change a generation. I believe that. But we've got to figure out how to do it, how to implement it.
>
> —JUSTIN, Montana educator

Justin and I typically met in his classroom after the school day. Our lengthy conversations frequently would last well into the late afternoon and early evening. Amid the lighthearted banter, jokes, and humorous stories, our conversations would always arc toward solemn considerations of Native education, reservation schools, and American Indian students. The school sits in a valley ringed with hills, and as we talked, the western hills would inevitably cast lonely shadows into the empty classroom. The very ambiance encouraged deep reflection. As the room grew increasingly darker, it seemed to me that Justin's contemplation tended to take on a more serious character. Perhaps it was merely my imagination, or possibly it merely reflected my own mood.

During one of our conversations, Justin used just five sentences to summarize the tragedy of American Indian education, the challenge facing Native educators, and the promise of reservation schools when he said, "I think school is a place where the culture was taken away from them. So I think school is a place where it can be brought back. Teach these kids the culture and change a generation. I believe that. But we've got to figure out how to do it, how to implement it." I found it to be a profound statement.

To say that Native children need highly qualified Native educators is to say the obvious. Yet, this truism is far from reality, given the few American Indian educators serving in reservation classrooms. Even when the classroom is staffed with a Native teacher who understands the cultural needs of American Indian students, the lack of culturally relevant curriculum can prove frustrating. Yet, in spite of all of this, reservation schools can, and in the minds of the six participants, will provide crucial cultural continuity for their communities. If American Indian educators are the instruments that will build the tribal strengths of Native nations, then it is reservation schools that must be the institutions to provide the means.

## Perspectives from Scholars

Well into adulthood many people have strong and specific memories of their teachers. Curiously, they often have similar recollections of their former schools, often referring to them as if they were living organisms. Indeed in many respects, schools are living organisms. They are social systems complete with their own local cultures, customs, fads, humor, urban legends, and histories. Little wonder people carry robust, vivid memories many years after leaving their school.

Systemically and institutionally, schools powerfully impact students. A review of the literature reveals two prevailing themes on how schools, on an institutional level, impact American Indian students and American Indian communities. First, researchers have examined the nature of the educational experience against persistence and attrition rates of Native students. Several theoretical perspectives on American Indian education have emerged from these pursuits and offer differing pictures of educational outcomes for Native students. Second, in recent years scholars have initiated serious examinations of ways in which schools can work to strengthen Native communities. Most notable in this regard are efforts to preserve the tribal legacy of Native nations. These scholarly exertions point out an ironic development in American Indian education, namely, historically policymakers and educators used schools to help eradicate tribal cultures; today we seek to employ schools in the effort to preserve tribal cultures.

THEORETICAL PERSPECTIVES ON AMERICAN INDIAN EDUCATION

For decades scholars and educators have lamented the lack of educational achievement among Native students. But many American Indian students experience tremendous educational accomplishments and go on to make significant contributions. Why do some American Indian students experience educational success and so many others encounter debilitating frustration that leads them not to flourish? Is there something uniquely different about the educational experiences of Native students that separate them from the educational experiences of other American minority students? What factors serve to inhibit academic success for Native students? Conversely, what are the key factors that facilitate educational achievement? Questions such as these persist in the American Indian education literature. But what is more, attempts to answer such questions have resulted in a number of important theoretical perspectives. Generally, scholars work from one of four theoretical frameworks to explain the nature of educational persistence and attrition among Native precollege students.[1] These theoretical perspectives include cultural discontinuity theory (the most dominant framework found in American Indian education scholarship), structural inequality theory and critical race theory (two very similar theoretical frameworks), and transculturation theory (unique in the fact that it developed specifically as a framework to explain American Indian educational experiences). Each of these perspectives contains a different premise and set of assumptions. Just as important, each perspective leads to different conclusions about the nature of academic success and disappointment among Native students. They share in common the attempt to unravel the intricacies of educational outcomes for American Indian students.

Cultural discontinuity theory is the most commonly used theoretical perspective found in American Indian education studies (Huffman, 2010). Like so many other theoretical frameworks employed by American Indian education scholars, cultural discontinuity theory did not originate as a way to explain Native education outcomes. Rather it developed as a means to account for the academic experiences of minority students in general. Nevertheless, scholars quickly employed it in the campaign to understand factors associated with Native educational success and failure. Essentially, cultural discontinuity theory attributes the lack of general educational achievement as due to differences in communication and interactional styles distinctly found in Native homes and those expected in formal classrooms of schools. As leading cultural discontinuity theorist Kathryn Au explains, "the theory of cultural discontinuity centers on a possible mismatch between the culture of the school and the culture of the home, which results in misunderstandings between teachers and students in the classroom" (1993, p. 8). Simply put, when it comes to ways of communicating (e.g., talking, listening, and responding) and anticipated normative behavior (e.g., eye contact, self-assertive demonstrations), Native parents and their children employ fundamentally different styles and nuances from those used by school teachers and administrators. The result of such incongruence is predictable—Native students are placed at a distinct disadvantage. Thus, academic achievement for Native students lags behind compared with those students whose previous socialization has prepared them to be more culturally congruent with the communication and interaction patterns prevailing in the mainstream institution.

Cultural discontinuity researchers have produced a host of scholarship. Susan Philips's work on Oregon's Warm Springs reservation represents the most well-known research from the cultural discontinuity perspective. Her ethnographic study of classroom dynamics of four elementary classrooms (two enrolling all Native students on the reservation and two enrolling predominately non-Native students at a nearby off-reservation community) resulted in the widely cited book *The Invisible Culture: Communication and Community on the Warm Springs Reservation* (1983), and scholars acknowledge it as an exemplar of the cultural discontinuity tradition (Huffman, 2010; Ledlow, 1992). Philips argued that communication and interaction patterns are learned before Native students enter school and are established by age six. As a result, American Indian children enter mainstream schools and classrooms as culturally foreign to the expectations held by most, if not all, of their teachers. This disadvantage, she points out, is not shared by white children. According to Philips, cultural misunderstandings emerge virtually immediately and only compound as the school year (and, presumably, school years ahead) continue. The consequences for Native students and families are serious. She concludes:

> Warm Springs Indian children learn socially appropriate ways of conveying attention and regulating turns at talk in their homes and their

community before they come to school . . . And they are deliberately socialized so that they acquire skills in the use of visual and auditory channels of communication in culturally distinctive ways. Thus in regard to both the structuring of attention and the allocation of turns at talk, Warm Springs Indian children learn culturally distinctive systems for socially appropriate communication.

At the age of six, the Indian children enter a classroom where the organization of interaction is Anglo in its hierarchical structure, and in the control of talk that one individual exercises. The relative use of the visual and auditory channels and the organization of participant structures for the presentation of curriculum have been developed for the Anglo middle-class child. The organization of classroom interaction at the first-grade level is designed to fit with or build on the interactional skills the Anglo children have acquired during their first six years of life. That organization does not, however, completely fit or build on the interactional skills acquired by the Warm Springs Indian children . . . Those differences contribute to the general uncertainty Indian children experience as they find they do not understand the teacher, and the teacher does not understand them. (1983, pp. 126–27)

Since Philips's groundbreaking study, cultural discontinuity theorists have gone on to identify a myriad of cultural misunderstandings plaguing Native students in mainstream classrooms. For instance, cultural incongruence leads to confusion regarding cultural tendencies toward cooperation over competitiveness (Amerman, 2007; Deyhle & LeCompte, 1994); tribal preference for personal reticence and aversion to self-assertiveness (Garrett, 1995; Little Soldier, 1997); and even discrepancies in learning styles between Native and non-Native students (Ingalls, Hammond, Dupoux, & Baeza, 2006; Pewewardy, 2002). For cultural discontinuity thinkers, cultural dissonance is actually a form of cultural conflict that eats away at the self-esteem, self-worth, and sense of purpose and identity of Native students (Jackson, Smith, & Hill, 2003; Sanders, 1987). Ultimately, the cultural conflict resulting from cultural incongruence is the leading reason for the lack of academic achievement among American Indian students at all levels of the educational system (Reyhner, 1992; Romero-Little, 2010; Ward, 2005). Indeed, leading American Indian education scholar Jon Reyhner (1992), in unflinching criticism of schools serving Native children, has argued, "Academically capable American Indian students often drop out of school because their needs are not being met. Others are pushed out because they protest, in a variety of ways, how they are being treated . . . American schools are not providing an appropriate education for Indian students who are put in large, factory-like schools. Indian students are denied teachers with special training in Indian education, denied a curriculum that includes their heritage, and denied culturally appropriate assessment. Their parents are also denied a voice in the education of their children" (p. 37).

For cultural discontinuity scholars, to correct the lack of educational success, schools must adopt culturally responsive approaches to education, particularly culturally appropriate pedagogy and relevant curriculum (Demmert, 2011; Gregory, 2013; Van Hamme, 1996). Lovelace and Wheeler (2006) argue that teachers need to recognize the responsibility to bridge cultures for their Native students and become cultural mediators. Further, they must proactively create cultural continuity between the learning that occurs in the homes of minority students and the learning that takes place in their classrooms. They must adopt flexible teaching techniques that allow for the ebb and flow of communication styles and patterns among all the students in the classroom. Unfortunately, strict curricular and pedagogical requirements resulting from assessment and educational policy mandates frustrate such teaching agility suggested by Lovelace and Wheeler. Further, the lack of teacher training required to recognize, understand, and work with culturally diverse learners constitutes a serious problem (Moeller, Anderson, & Grosz, 2012; Morgan, 2009).

Both structural inequality theory and critical race theory contrast sharply to cultural discontinuity theory. Traditionally, scholars consider these two theories as distinct (owing to an important difference); yet, they also share a similar premise and set of assumptions. Structural inequality theory has a longer history in American Indian education studies compared with critical race theory. As such, a larger body of research produced by structural inequality scholars is found in the American Indian education literature. Indeed, perhaps because of its longer history, critical race scholars frequently cite the work of earlier structural inequality theorists. Nevertheless, today scholars appear to prefer the basic tenets of critical race theory, and thus, it is becoming the more dominant perspective of the two frameworks (Huffman, 2010).

For structural inequality theorists, the lack of educational success among many minority students is not due to cultural differences between the home and the classroom that work against them; rather, the very way in which society is structured is the true barrier to academic achievement. Essentially, societies, such as the United States, are organized in such a manner that they inherently provide unequal access to resources and opportunities to different social groups (Au, 1993; Ogbu, 1978, 1987). As a result, over time those who have been granted greater access to those resources and opportunities gain larger advantages compared with those who have historically been denied access[2] (Ogbu & Simons, 1998).

Building on this fundamental premise, American Indian education studies scholars working out of the structural inequality tradition regard historically produced social structural conditions as barriers to academic success. They point to such powerful structural factors as the decades of assimilationist education policies that left behind a legacy of dispirited and suspicions attitudes toward mainstream education among reservation peoples (Nagel, 1996; Robinson-Zanartu & Majel-Dixon, 1996; Wood & Clay, 1996); the inefficient and misguided management of Native education resulting in a disjoined patchwork of different types of schools serving Native children (C. Ward, 2005; Wilkinson, 2005); and inadequate funding of reservation schools, which frequently places American Indian students at a distinct advantage compared with non-Native students attending better-funded systems (Cleary & Peacock, 1998; Senese, 1991). Even current standardized assessment techniques are culturally slanted in favor of dominant group students (Forbes, 2000). For structural inequality theorists, the net result is that education operates primarily to serve the interests of the most powerful and dominant in society at the expense of American Indian students. Thus, correcting cultural discontinuities in the classroom will do nothing to erase basic inequalities structured into society itself (Ogbu, 1982). Given these formidable obstacles, little wonder American Indian academic achievement falters behind that of non-Natives (Ledlow, 1992; St. Germaine, 1995; Wood & Clay, 1996).

Like structural inequality theorists, critical race theorists reject the notion that discrepancies in linguistic and behavioral styles found in the classroom account for the gap in educational achievement between Native and non-Native students. Critical race theorists too accept the premise that larger social arrangements powerfully determine the social conditions of people's lives. The fundamental difference between structural inequality theory and critical race theory is their departure over

the basis for social inequalities in society. For structural inequality theorists, social inequalities derive from prevailing economic conditions
that powerfully separate people into social strata and determine much
of their opportunities for success—academic and otherwise (Au, 1993;
Wood & Clay, 1996). Thus, entrenched reservation and urban poverty is
the result of capitalist forces that operate to the advantage of those with
political power and economic leverage and against tribal nations. For
critical race theorists, race is the most powerful factor in separating people into social groups. Indeed, according to these scholars, race is even
more powerful than economic standing (Crenshaw, Gotanda, Peller, &
Thomas, 1995; Delgado & Stefancic, 2001). Critical race theorists regard
racism as a normative state in society, not a social aberration. As a result,
racial group membership provides inherent privileges to some and denies
them to others. In effect, wealth is no guarantee against discriminatory
attitudes and behaviors when racial status trumps economic status.
Thus, an important implication is that race does matter in all levels of
public policy (including educational policy), and notions of color-blind
objectivity are both unrealistic as well as potentially harmful[3] (Delgado
& Stefancic, 2001).

Critical race theorists regard established cultural norms and standards
as written by the dominant group for their benefit and perpetual advantage. Essentially, white Americans have written the cultural narratives
organizing society, and these narratives have largely gone unchallenged.
As a result, "white privilege" serves to powerfully benefit white people
by providing subtle and frequently unrecognized advantages, including
higher social status as well as greater economic and educational opportunities (McIntosh, 2006; Rothenberg, 2005). Significantly, white privilege
also involves a generalized acceptance of white Americans' experiences,
especially concerning equal opportunity, as normal and universal to all
others in society (Ladson-Billings, 1999; Martin-McDonald & McCarthy, 2008). Thus, a major task facing critical race scholars is to provide
"counternarratives" to expose the fallacies and inconsistencies contained
in the prevailing narratives that serve to protect white privilege (Laughter,
Baker, Williams, Cearley, & Milner, 2006; Vaught & Castagno, 2008).
These counternarratives tell the social and personal stories of minority
members and ensure that their experiential knowledge is revealed (Chandler & McKnight, 2008; Solorzano & Yosso, 2002).

Critical race theory has splintered into a variety of perspectives, each attempting to account for the specific experiences of racial groups (Delgado & Stefancic, 2001). For instance, the scholarly literature now contains Asian critical race theory and Latino/a critical race theory. This separation into specific theoretical strands makes sense. If race is the primary factor in determining social location, circumstances, and opportunities, it is also logical to assume that each racial group has its own unique history and personal narratives that require specific treatment. Bryan Brayboy (2005) introduced such a variety of critical race theory as a means to examine and present American Indian experiences—tribal critical race theory.

As the name implies, tribal critical race theory (or, as Brayboy refers to it, "TribalCrit") attempts to present the counternarratives unique among Native peoples. At the heart of tribal critical race theory is the notion that Eurocentric cultural and political colonization has and continues to dominate the lives of Native nations and individuals (Rains, 2002). To understand the complexities of Native lives, therefore, one must begin to appreciate the overwhelming nature of this colonial domination. Brayboy relates, "The primary tenet of TribalCrit is the notion that colonization is endemic to society. By colonization, I mean that European American thought, knowledge, and power structures dominate present-day society in the United States . . . In this way the goal sometimes explicit, sometimes implicit, on interactions between the dominant US society and American Indians has been to change ('colonize' or 'civilize') us to be more like those who hold power in the dominant society" (2005, p. 430).

A review of the literature reveals that tribal critical race theory is frequently used in three ways: to frame the dynamics of community responses to racially charged situations, to examine how Native students experience mainstream education, and to explore ways in which teachers can better respond to the unique personal histories of American Indian students (Rains, 2003).

Matthew Fletcher (2008) used tribal critical race theory to demonstrate how injudicious educational policy decisions led to disastrous consequences for a Native community. The counternarratives contained in his work provide a way to understand the experiences and perceptions of Native people facing a complex legal struggle over autonomy of local schools and the resistance to directives believed to erode tribal cultural integrity. His effort illustrates how tribal critical race theory can be used to explore and understand the manner in which an American Indian community responded to what the residents regarded as unfair treatment.

Scholars have most frequently applied tribal critical race theory to examine the higher educational experiences of Native students as opposed to precollege students. Nevertheless, these efforts offer insight on the use of tribal identities and strengths among American Indians (Cueva, 2013). For instance, in tribal critical race theory research with American Indian female teacher candidates in the Southwestern United States, Writer and Oesterreich (2011) tell the stories of the students' "struggles with and resistance to institutional inequality and oppression" (p. 509). Their work documents how these individuals, rather than being "at risk," regarded themselves as women "with strength." The researchers, along with their participants, used the findings "to challenge and transform the higher education institution to secure a reality of degreed community-based educators" (p. 509).

Tribal critical race theory also helps inform educators on appropriate ways to teach American Indian students (Grande, 2004; Roithmayr, 1999). Chandler (2011) outlined ways in which educators can use critical race theory to teach American Indian history and, thereby, achieve a different (and frequently hidden) understanding of Native nations within the United States. Scholarly offerings such as these reveal how tribal critical race theory can be used to broaden the viewpoints of students and lead to fuller appreciation of Native/US history than provided in traditional educational perspectives.

Among the theoretical perspectives frequently used by American Indian education scholars, transculturation theory is unique. It is the only theoretical perspective that developed specifically as a way to explain educational achievement among Native students[4] (Huffman, 2010). In addition, transculturation theory attempts to explore the reasons why American Indian students succeed academically rather than concentrating on the factors associated with a lack of success (White Shield, 2009). These features of the theory represent important departures from much of the past scholarly work in American Indian education studies (Huffman, 2010; Okagaki et al., 2009).

Essentially, transculturation theory asserts that the key to educational achievement for Native students lies in their tribal identity. Its premise asserts that a strong tribal identity combined with a salient value system grounded in tribal worldview and culture provide the confidence necessary to navigate through mainstream educational institutions. For example, Rosemary White Shield (2009) used transculturation theory as a conceptual framework to explore the higher educational experiences of eight tribally traditional American Indian undergraduate and graduate women.[5] She found four significant experiences shared by the women in her study. First, spirituality played a highly instrumental role in helping the women traverse through the demands of higher education. Second, they used the tribal traditions and wisdom of their people as sources of inspiration and guidance. Third, the individuals found tremendous sustaining power in the traditional roles for women. Although those roles varied according to distinct tribal traditions, they nevertheless discovered a sense of purpose and commitment resulting from their Native womanhood. Fourth, strengths derived from their family were crucial to their educational success. Their academic accomplishments were not regarded as individual achievements but rather a success shared by the entire family.

White Shield's work demonstrates the critical importance of tribal strengths in the academic pursuits of tribally oriented American Indians. She documented specific ways in which tribal strengths (both in the form of tribal identity and tribal legacy) work to the advantage of Native individuals. In summarizing her findings, White Shield concludes:

> The results of this study showed that the cultural and spiritual strengths of Native women completing a higher education experience were grounded in their sense of reliance on a power or powers greater than themselves. These strengths manifested themselves in forms that were tribally congruent with Native value systems and definitions of reality. Utilization of these strengths was the core and primary means whereby the participants achieved their goals. Congruent with Huffman's transculturation theory, this sense of "Indianness" was not transferred into them by external sources, but was a result of self-discovery within a Native cultural context. Throughout the process of completing a higher educational experience, the participant's sense of purpose was a commitment to their Nations, their people, and their families. This sense of love for their people, and for their families enabled them to move beyond the "odds" and make the impossible possible. (p. 62)

The conceptual notion of tribal strengths is closed linked to the theoretical idea of transculturation (which is the key concept found in transculturation theory). The notion of tribal strengths is embedded in the idea Sitting Bull had in mind all those years ago when he declared "but we will retain our beauty and still be Indians." Today that same process that allows for a person to utilize his/her tribal strengths is given a name—transculturation. Previously, I have defined transculturation in this way: "the process by which an individual can enter and interact in the milieu of another culture without loss of the person's native cultural identity and ways" (Huffman, 2008, p. 147). Although similar to the commonly used concept of biculturation, transculturation is conceptually different. And that difference between the two concepts is crucial for transculturation theorists (Huffman, 2010). The fundamental difference is that biculturation traditionally has come to mean that an individual adds and subtracts cultural elements in order to interact in and between two cultural settings. The notion of transculturation makes no such assumption. In this conception, a person only adds cultural elements; no need exists to relinquish cultural elements to make room for new cultural traits. Thus, as Sitting Bull would have put it, a person retains his/her cultural beauty.

It is also important to keep in mind that transculturation is a process, akin to a cultural journey. A person never arrives as a cultural hybrid (as it implied in biculturation) (Huffman et al., 1986) but is continually learning, unlearning, and relearning cultural nuances of various cultural settings. As a result, a person's cultural identity is constantly being constructed and deconstructed. However, as a result of this cycle, the transcultured individual uses the strength of his/her tribal identity as a personal anchor and thus endures the vicissitudes that accompany the process of navigating back and forth between mainstream and tribal communities. For example, examining the process of moving between cultural settings necessary for a group of Montana American Indian college students, Davis (1992), using transculturation theory as an analytic framework, documented the use of tribal identity as the key to academic success. As she relates, "These students were able to retain their Indian culture, to be Indian, and to be a successful student in the middle-class system" (p. 29).

I too was able to document the powerful use of tribal strengths as a means to facilitate academic achievement. In a five-year study involving personal interviews with sixty-nine American Indian college students, I found that a strong tribal identity was essential for success in college for those with a tribally traditional orientation (Huffman, 2001, 2008). What is especially important is that virtually all of these students experienced extremely difficult introductions to college. Many struggled for years with bouts of cultural conflict, depression, academic difficulties, and a variety of personal hardships. Yet, their tribal identities, a sense of purpose derived from their tribal heritage, and nurturing drawn from traditional family relationships proved critical in sustaining them through the demands of mainstream higher education. In other words, their tribal strengths provided the crucial factor to persistence and eventual college graduation.

Transculturation is internally derived. That is, it emerges within an individual and not a cultural transformation imposed by external forces. Essentially, the decision to use one's ethnic identity as an anchor is a personal choice. My research with transculturated Native college students revealed that most students arrived at a specific point at which they made a deliberate, personal choice to use their ethnicity to frame values and guide their behaviors. I referred to this point in their cultural journey as the "transculturated threshold."

Okagaki et al. (2009) used transculturation theory to examine the relationship between tribal identity and academic outcomes. Their quantitative study found strong evidence for the linkage between a strong tribal identity and educational success. Moreover, they assert that persistence and achievement in college emerges directly from one's use of tribal identity. They argue, "Our findings appear to corroborate Huffman's (2001) findings that students who have a strong identification for their American Indian culture and an openness (but not assimilationist view) to the majority culture appear to have positive education related beliefs and experiences . . . The findings from our study appear to support Huffman's (2001) findings and suggest that students who believe that they can be true to their ethnic identity and draw strength from it while facing the challenges of campus life may be more likely to succeed in their academic pursuits." (p. 172).

Common among all these theoretical perspectives is that they point to the importance of tribal strengths in the educational careers of Native students. Further, they suggest the importance of schools as institutions in reinforcing the tribal strengths of American Indians (Lysne & Levy, 1997). Tribal strengths help define an individual as culturally unique and serve to anchor his/her personal identity, value system, and even worldview. In the realm of education, leaning into tribal strengths can potentially serve American Indian students in three crucial ways. It can help facilitate a strong identity, enhance a feeling of connectedness, and provide a sense of purpose.

Perhaps one of the most powerful dynamics of the academic experience for Native students is the impact school can have on one's personal cultural/tribal identity. It is absolutely critical that Native students be encouraged and allowed to embrace, express, and celebrate their own ethnicity. If anything is clear, research has firmly established the important link between a strong American Indian identity and academic achievement (Deyhle, 1994; Horse, 2005; Huffman, 2001, 2008; Huffman et al., 1986; Lomawaima & McCarty, 2006; Okagaki et al., 2009; Whitbeck et al., 2001; White Shield, 2009).

A feeling of connectedness is complex and multidimensional. Connectedness relates to relationships with one's own family and community. It also relates to a student's relationship with the school and its staff. I believe one of the most ignored aspects of the academic experience for Native students is the desire to feel connected to the institution and its people. There has been consistent research over the last thirty years documenting the need for Native students to make a personal connection with staff and especially faculty (Coladarci, 1983; Falk & Aitken, 1984; Garrett, Bellon-Harn, Torres-Rivera, Garrett, & Roberts, 2003; Huffman, 2008).

Everyone needs a direction in life. During my own career I have witnessed how many Native students appear motivated by a set of values different from those that drive many non-Native students. This is especially so among American Indian students from reservation areas who often desire to make significant contributions to their people. Perhaps it is for that reason we frequently find Native college students majoring in fields leading them into some sort of community service.[6] It is important for educators to emphasize ways in which the specific subject material they teach (as well as conveying how educational achievement in general) can be used for the larger good. Having a sense of greater purpose is a powerful motivator. And it can sustain Native students through difficult times

(Huffman, 2011; Jackson et al., 2003; Juntunen et al., 2001; Pavel et al., 2002; White Shield, 2009; Zahrt, 2001).

SCHOOLS AND NATIVE COMMUNITIES

For good reasons, the checkered history of formal, Western-styled education among tribal nations has left a heavy residue of skepticism and distrust. American Indian education has long been (and continues to be) highly politicized and, thus, driven by a variety of agendas. Reflecting on this history, Native scholar Deirdre Almeida (1998) argues, "For Indigenous nations, education has been a political tool to deny them their identities as the first peoples of the land and to eliminate their sovereignty rights to govern themselves and their lands" (p. 7).

But as the result of determined and courageous effort, change is occurring. Even in the face of daunting policy mandates and heavy-handed sanctioning procedures, Native and non-Native educators and leaders are finding means allowing reservation schools to operate in ways that strengthen Native communities (Boyer, 2006). For instance, increasingly, educators recognize the strengths and importance of Native families (HeavyRunner & DeCelles, 2002). Building trust through genuine respect and open communication, educators demonstrate their desire to truly work with and rely on families (Pewewardy & Fitzpatrick, 2009).

Leaders of reservation schools are also coming to appreciate the cultural needs of their students along with those of the larger community. Growing awareness of the importance of addressing these needs (combined with a growing understanding of how tribal identity is connected to academic success) can be found in an increasing number of reservation schools. As Martinez (2014) observes, "American Indian students need to develop a strong sense of both their tribal identity and also their academic identity. They must view their cultural identity as being compatible with a positive academic identity. Students who have a strong cultural identification and can successfully operate in a majority culture have the most positive educational outcomes. Academic success does not need to detract from strong cultural identity. School cultures that are more congruent [with] tribal values will better serve the needs of American Indian students . . . Education is a pathway of many journeys; schools that embrace tribal values can be an important part of this journey" (p. 204).

William Ruff (2014) used a comparative case study to examine ways in which two effective reservation schools infuse tribal epistemologies and leadership practices to serve local students and communities. One school had documented high levels of student achievement as measured by standardized testing assessments, whereas the other school demonstrated persistent increases in student achievement over a period of three years. As part of the case study methodology, Ruff and his research associate observed classroom instruction, school-wide routines, and interactions of students with tribal elders. Additionally, the researchers conducted semistructured interviews with the principals and leadership teams of the schools.

Ruff reported important similarities in these reservation schools in the manner in which they serve children and the community. Common to both schools was a strong connection to their communities and genuine respect and application of tribal values and traditions. Moreover, these traits were personally modeled in the lives and leadership of the principals. "Both schools had American Indian principals with deep connections with the community, demonstrated tribal traditions, and enacted leadership best practice models . . . The principals both practiced the traditions of their tribes and participated in ceremonies on a regular basis. Like many other successful schools with large proportions of American Indian students, school practices incorporated tribal language and tradition into daily routines and instruction. Yet, a difference between these schools and other schools was seen in the degree of personalization. This personalization connected students with traditions and facilitated a strong sense of identity that seemed to be fostered by the principals' sense of identity" (2014, p. 19).

Beyond the deliberate effort to shape the leadership style and institutional values found in the school to align with those of the community, the principals attempted to positively impact the reservation by creating a shared identity and vision within the school itself. Ruff explains, "As demonstrated in the converging themes found in this comparative case study, there was a clear and deep conviction in the identity of the principals with community identity. The principals effectively met the expectations of the community and championed the identity of the school within the larger community context. These school leaders created identity within the school through facilitating a shared vision among faculty, staff and students as well as enabling action toward the shared vision. Furthermore, there was evidence that the norms and values of the school were beginning to reshape the norms and values of the community" (2014, p. 20).

The use of reservation schools to help preserve tribal culture is a theme frequently found in the literature. In an ironic twist of history, increasingly reservation schools (rather than seen as instruments of forced cultural assimilations) are being relied on to help preserve tribal cultures and languages (Freedman, 2011; Huffman, 2013). Some register reasonable hesitancy over specific aspects of these efforts (e.g., concerns surrounding the appropriate teaching and use of tribal spiritual knowledge) (Begaye, 2007; Márquez Lavine, 2011; Pewewardy, 1998b; Ward, 2011; Woodrum, 2009). Nevertheless, a large number of political leaders, educators, parents, and tribal elders welcome the inclusion of tribal history and language in schools as a necessary step toward cultural preservation. Montana State representative and Mandan/Hidatsa member Carol Juneau (2006) contends, "Indian people have understood for a great many years that it is only by educating our young people that we can reclaim our history and only through culturally responsive education that we will preserve our cultural integrity" (p. 217). Expressing similar sentiments, Northern Cheyenne elder Lynwood Tall Bull (2006) suggests, "Every tribe in Montana and throughout the United States has a colorful, interesting history, strong stories and legends, knowledge about plants and healing, and survival skills. Knowing more about each other will help non-Indian and Indian children learn to live together well. When we start to learn more about Indian history and culture, all children in our schools will be getting an education about the best of both worlds" (p. 192).

There can be little doubt about the urgency of the situation. Of the approximately close to seven thousand languages spoken in the world today, it is estimated that over half will be extinct by the end of the century (Hornberger, 2008). Virtually all endangered languages are Indigenous languages, and more than a few belong to North American tribal nations. As such, many Native educators feel a special responsibility to help stem the loss of language and the culture it holds. In a study on how Native educators understand the inclusion of tribal culture in the classroom, Begaye (2007) reports, "Some teachers expressed concern about the current state of their language by noting that in their communities the only means of preserving the language today is through schools and institutions that originally prevented its use" (p. 43).

Beyond the obvious contribution toward cultural preservation, the inclusion of tribal culture and language in schools is seen to have two other major benefits. First, Native educators report tremendous intrinsic rewards from assisting to preserve the cultural heritage of the tribe and believe this is an essential responsibility (Cherubini et al., 2009; Cherubini et al., 2010; Hill et al., 1995; Huffman, 2013; Kitchen et al., 2011). Additionally, research evidence demonstrates that tribal preservation inclusion in reservation schools directly benefits academic success for Native students. Namely, such efforts serve to reinforce the tribal identity for American Indian youths and lead to greater cultural pride (Almeida, 1998; Begaye, 2007; Márquez Lavine, 2011; Martinez, 2014; Ward, 2011). As Monique Fordham (1998) explains, "It appears that the revival of Indigenous languages as part of education helps to ground Native peoples in a sense of pride and identity, encouraging achievement and self-expression throughout the generations" (p. 44).

## Voices from the Reservation Classroom

The six educators held strong opinions on how reservation schools can serve Native students and communities. Their views often align with the perspectives of scholars found in the professional literature. They too regarded a strong tribal emphasis in the instruction and operation of the school as crucial to the academic success of students. They also believed that reservation schools can and must play a critical role in tribal preservation efforts. They especially saw great potential for schools to assist in tribal language revitalization.

Two general themes surrounding the perceptions on the tribal strengths of reservation schools stand out from the interviews. First, the educators emphasized that reservation schools must operate in ways that consistently fortify the tribal strengths (especially the tribal identity) of American Indian students. Second, they are convinced that reservation schools must function to preserve tribal culture and language. However, they also believed that much of this work has to be informal and interpersonal, whereby Native educators demonstrate tribal values and worldviews to their students.

## FORTIFYING THE TRIBAL STRENGTHS OF
## AMERICAN INDIAN STUDENTS

The contention that reservation schools can function to fortify the existing and potential tribal strengths of American Indian students was expressed in a variety of ways. For instance, both Justin and Rachel believed reservation schools can help Native students understand and deal with racism. For Justin, the approach is more formal and involves deliberate curricular initiatives. He saw Montana's Indian Education for All as an important tool to help alleviate racial tensions and misunderstandings. Yet he was also realistic about the limitations involved in combating historically entrenched racial attitudes. Justin reasoned:

> I think Indian Education for All is kind of addressing that [racism]. It helps people understand what happened to the Native people. It's not common knowledge, it's not part of your textbook history. That real history portrays America in a very negative light once you understand what happened. Just going in and taking somebody's stuff, there's something morally wrong about that. But, it's like, how deep do teachers get into it? I'm sure in Missoula it's more than it is in say eastern Montana. I think part of it probably depends on the community. Your more liberal communities are probably more open to teaching certain perspectives and saying, "This was wrong. This is what happened, but it was wrong." Whereas, in your more conservative areas of the state, they are not too excited about exploring the subject. I think the important thing with Indian Education for All is, it's got to be an in-depth conversation. There's some serious racial issues in Montana. Especially in places like border towns. There's still some racial tension in certain places, and hopefully Indian Education for All does some things where some of those stereotypes are knocked down and people start to realize and see people for people.

Rachel clearly took a highly personal approach to preparing her students for encounters with racism. As she weighed the challenges before them, she carefully crafted a personal response designed to help Native students confront negative racial attitudes and behaviors:

> I always try to teach them how to deal with negative attitudes. I say, "When you play basketball and you go someplace, to these other bordering towns—they're going to treat you bad; they're going to say things to make you mad. Don't let them do that to you. You hear them but just ignore them. Brush it off. Because they're going to do that. They're doing it to get a reaction from you." So, I always try to teach them how to deal

with the racism because it's going to happen. As much as I hate to say it, we haven't changed much in this country. And with Obama and the presidency, you just see it getting worse! But I think it's all right if our kids, you know, if we can teach them to look at themselves and be happy about who they are. Be proud of who they are. Be proud of where they come from and that they're still connected. Today's going to be different from what tomorrow will bring. But everything's changing—even our ceremonies, and our language—but it's still there, and we can still connect to it. We can still teach it.

Assisting students to cope with racism is closely associated with building strong tribal identities. Rachel related as much when she continued, "I think our being connected to who we are is absolute. It's just like with my kids, I'll say, 'It don't matter what they call you, or what they say. They call you dog-eaters; they make fun of you. You know who you are; you're Lakota. You're Native American. Be proud of who you are. Don't let anybody ever make you feel bad about who you are.'"

Moreover, the educators believed that working to fortify the tribal strengths of Native students requires a grounding in essential tribal values. Even simple expressions of crucial tribal values prove invaluable to equipping American Indian youth. As Donna explained, "The first and foremost is respect. I mean, that has to be there for us. And it's a two-way street. That's the first thing we concentrate on. That very first month of school, that's the first thing that we concentrate on. I mean, even staff, you know, at our staff meetings, we talk about the importance of demonstrating respect as a Lakota value to each other and our students."

Lori also suggested that reservation schools must do more than merely offer tribal cultural activities; tribal cultural heritage must also be made relevant and meaningful in order to impact the lives of Native students. While she acknowledged the variety of cultural activities available to students, she also warned of the potential for disconnection between cultural events and what they truly represent. Lori clearly realized that tribal strengths must have real meaning in the lives of students. She related, "There's still a lot of cultural activity out there that our kids could participate in. And they do. We also bring some of that into our school, but I don't think they've quite made that connection why it's so important. But there are a lot of things. There are some things that we're trying to do to instill that now back into their minds so they realize that, 'Yeah, this is who I am and this is why it's so important.'"

Ben offered the most poignant observations on the need for reservation schools to fortify the tribal strengths of Native students. As previously noted, Ben's school had suffered though the horrible tragedies of student suicides. Indeed, all six of the educators had experienced the trauma of suicides among their students and even their staff. The freshness and the sheer number of these heartbreaking losses staggered Ben and his staff. The urgency to respond to the needs of his people is clearly evident in Ben's reflection on that dramatic moment in his career when a series of student suicides clustered together and he recognized that only the tribal strengths of the nation could suffice. Yet, he struggled with the controversies associated with reservation schools fully committing to the spirituality central to tribal strengths.

We're culturally relevant, but we don't do too much on the cultural end of it because I think we're scared to offend people, we're scared to offend parents, we're scared to do the wrong thing. We're aware of the culturally relevant piece, but what we do is, we do enough to be safe. But we don't do enough to get kids really in tune to where they come from. And I think a big part of it is not only we don't know how but we're afraid that we might offend someone. Let me give you a good example. When we had the suicides we were sort of at our wit's end, and we didn't know what in the hell to do. And I think this will really, really help you understand where the school stands in terms of the cultural relevance. So I remember sitting in this office and we were like, "Boy, what do we do?" We didn't know what to do. We had a crisis team that was called, obviously. And me? I was pretty shook up. I didn't know where to turn or anything. So we put together a plan. We're going to bring in some elders from the community, and we're going to offer the opportunity to smudge. We're going to have a prayer in school. So we broke every law in the book. And we're going to talk about who we are, we're going talk about where we're going to go, and we're going to emphasize the praying end of it. Who we pray to, why we pray. And we brought the elders in; took them down to the gym; had an assembly. It was an emergency assembly. And we smudged; we prayed; told the kids why we're doing it. And then we had one tribal board member who's a really traditional guy, and he helped a lot. And so we broke every rule in the book. But we didn't know what to do. We were in a crisis situation. We felt that was the only thing at that point to do. So we got those students, some of them for the first time, in touch with who they are. We explained to them what we were doing, and I'll tell you what, it was an eye-opening experience and probably one of the proudest things I've ever done. Those kids, for the first time, truly got to see and experience a powerful thing as to what your culture can do for you. What the spirituality within your culture can do for you. And they came to see really why we need to do it. Why we have to do this, why we have to get back to those type of things. And since then, we haven't had people kill themselves. We haven't had any kids now. I'll tell you what, when those kids were in there doing it, for me there was not a more powerful thing in terms of our mission statement or being culturally relevant, because not only was it culturally relevant, but it was the core of one of the practices of who we are, why we do it. And, of course, the state would throw a fit. We didn't know what else to do.

Ultimately, Ben resolved his ambivalence and took the courageous step to continue to rely on tribal spirituality to provide a sense of purpose and direction (as well as enhance the tribal identity) for his students. He became committed to the belief that tribal strengths, in all its expressions, is a powerful force in the lives of Native students. In Ben's case, it was the reservation school that became the proper arena for tribal strengths to become alive and real for American Indian youths:

> And if we could offer more of those kind of things, I think our students, not only would they get in touch with who they are, but I think it would help for them to provide a lot of direction when times get tough. Who do you turn to when things are going bad? Or where do you go when you pray? You sweat and you do all of that and it helps. It really does. It was a powerful thing. It really was. And we did it again a couple weeks later. We had another assembly. This time we just told kids if they wanted to, you can. Most of them did. And I think most of them felt real good about doing it. We prayed with them. And it's cultural teaching that a lot of them don't get anywhere else.

### PRESERVE TRIBAL STRENGTHS FOR THE FUTURE

Ben was hardly alone in his conviction that tribal spirituality is essential to the well-being and future of Native children. The educators, to a person, regarded tribal spirituality as a critical and inseparable component of tribal strengths. Clearly Donna, Rachel, and Lori did not struggle with ambivalent feelings regarding the place of tribal spirituality and reservation schools.[7] For them, spirituality is simply part of being a Native individual. As they regarded it, there is no need for controversy, because to the tribal nation, no controversy exists. Further, tribal spirituality must be protected and preserved for future generations. Perhaps Lori said it best:

When you talk about spiritualty, people cannot separate it from spiritualty as a Lakota person. It's how you live. It's being connected to everything in the universe. But other people who don't make that connection or understand that think of it as a religion, and it's not a religion. Spirituality is throughout the culture. It's that centeredness and knowing who you are and knowing where you came from and that you're related to everything. That's what, to me, what spirituality is. And so you don't have to separate it; you don't even [have] to use that word "spirituality." If you've been around the Lakota people for a long time, especially the traditional people, it is so a part of their life. They never exclude that out of their life, and that's where those values come from. You have a code of behavior that you have to follow. To me it's like when you live that life it's almost like you don't even have to use the word "spiritual." You have that sense that it's there. So I think you can teach that part. It's just getting past that word I think. It's in our Vision Statement, our vision here. And the school board members wanted it taken out. They said. "Are you talking about religion?" We said, "No, we're talking about a way of life." And that's kind of how we word it in our curriculum that we developed, to be at peace.

Rachel was even more direct in her views on tribal spirituality and reservation schools. She related that teaching about Lakota culture necessarily includes concepts on spirituality as a consistent and natural part of the nation's identity. Thus, it is not only acceptable but indispensable to socialize Lakota children into the full essence of their tribal strengths. As she explained:

I say, "Every morning on the way to work, I pray for you guys." Whether that's important or not? I think so; our spirituality—whether it is introduced to them through the school or through their families—it connects them. It connects all of us. One time, my daughter said that she smelled cedar burning somewhere. She said, "Oh, mom, it smells like Sun Dance time!" For us that's a real spiritual time. And it brings that connectedness right away. And we connect to that at work; we're part of that already. What we pray for that summer, what we pray for all year long—it brings it right to you. So, when we were talking about that this morning [in her class], I said, "That's who we are, as Native people. We're very spiritual people. When we pick the plants"—I said, "My children know, my own kids, that if they go out, they're going to pick sage; they make an offering, whether it's a prayer, or it's tobacco, or whether it's a song, you offer something back." I said, "Without the spirit, we would not survive, because she gives us our food; our plants; the animals live off her; they graze off her." I said, "Without her, we would not survive.

We need her" . . . So, the kids this morning—we were sitting, and just talking about spirituality. We talked about sage and stuff—burning it and stuff—before, but I really believe it's important. And we need to preserve that for the future. So the teaching here is important.

Rachel continued by discussing how reservation schools have the responsibility to assist in the preservation of tribal strengths. Responding to the question, "Can schools help preserve tribal culture and language?" she said:

> I think so. I think so. But it needs to be really pushed, and I don't push it as much because we're so NCLB [No Child Left Behind]. Academic, academic, academic! And that takes away from a lot of the time that we use to do things together. It's like, "Okay. I've got you guys on the MP3 player. I want you to listen to the Flag Song." And they have to listen to the Flag Song on there. There's so much you can do with them anymore: on the computer, on the CDs. They have the sentences so that they can speak the song; they can learn. And I like the songs, because you're learning a lot . . . So, I think the school can teach them that. We can learn that. I've seen my kids learn that. We had talking circles. The kids learned to pray, and pray for each other in that circle. "Okay, so, what's in your heart?" "I don't know how to pray," they'd say. "Yes, you do! Do you want it to be good?" "Yeah." "So, then, pray for it to be good. What do you want to happen, for things to be good for your mom?" And they'll say it. "Then, that's your prayer. That's your prayer; that's what you ask in your heart" I'd tell them. And I'd explain, "That's why we say the Lakota pray with their heart because they want what's good from their heart to help that person."

Justin emphasized the need for concerted, institutional effort to preserve tribal culture and language. But he also raised important questions regarding the qualification to legitimately teach tribal culture. Significantly, he acknowledged his own personal responsibility to prepare himself to lead young Native students into greater knowledge and awareness of their heritage:

> I see a lot of reservations are creating language schools and we don't have that here. That's one of the things I've thought, what if somebody did get that started? It gives those children an opportunity or an option. But on the other hand, the majority of the kids on the reservation go to school here. I'd like to see our school start to do some things like that. We got some grants and stuff right now. Hopefully, we'll start to see some more culture brought in, but then too, not all the educators understand the

history. I mean, from my elementary education classes, I didn't pick it up. In Native American studies, I went out and got 30 credits on my own, just because I thought that was beneficial to me as a person to understand that history. From that I got a cultural frame of reference. I can understand why things are the way they are and what can be done to try to get back some of that lost culture and that lost identity.

## Buildings, People, and the Stories They Tell

Sometimes a building is just a building. From the outside, it is a sad-looking affair. Sometimes a building is a symbol. A number of the windows are broken, grass grows uncut and unsightly around it, and the chain-link fence erected to keep intruders out does nothing to improve the looks. Sometimes a building prompts powerful emotions. The building sits in a valley at the base of a steep hill; the very location suggests a lowly existence and visually leaves one with an impression of its insignificance. Sometimes a building can tell stories, if we care to listen.

The building I am thinking about has lots of stories to tell.[8] It has a checkered history, and there are many opinions on what to do with the structure. It was constructed many decades ago, likely sometime between the World Wars, a "state of the art" building for the time. For decades it served as the main elementary school for the reservation and introduced scores of Native children into the formal education of the mainstream society. Early generations of its students were alienated by the heavy-handed assimilationist-guided educational strategies characteristic of most of the twentieth century. Many of its former students were left demoralized and cynical about the educational offerings of the school, a condition that sociologist Bruce Chadwick (1972) four decades ago referred to as the "inedible feast" of American Indian education.

But in time it also came to be headed by a local Native woman serving as principal, an individual, it should be noted, who gained a national reputation for leadership and innovation. She led the school into the turn of the twenty-first century. This was a heady time for the school, and for perhaps a decade and a half it was staffed with a number of highly qualified Native teachers, introduced culturally appropriate pedagogical practices, and won state, regional, and national acclaim. And then things changed. Staff left, retired, moved away, and a general state of decline and eventual inertia set in and became, dare I say it . . . accepted.

The mixed legacy of American Indian education attached itself to this particular building. And there it stands, a silent witness to the good and the bad associated with the history of Native education. The building is at once and the same time a symbol of cultural humiliation, tribal pride, and academic malaise. The stories this building tells depends on one's generation and one's perspective. But there are lots of stories to tell.

Yet, that is not the end of this particular story. Just a mile or so away a new school building sits on top of a hill with a commanding view of the reservation valley below. It is a beautiful facility, constructed in just the last few years. It is the product of concerted cooperation between the tribal government, the Bureau of Indian Education, and the state school district. Central to its mission is the recognition of the cultural integrity as well as the cultural preservation of the tribes it serves. Indeed, the very architecture of the building and the grounds were deliberately designed to reflect the tribal traditions of the nations of the reservation. The Native children who attend this school appear genuinely happy, and their academic and social needs are taken seriously by a highly qualified Native and non-Native staff. This building too has a promising story to tell. I am both excited and encouraged to think about how this new narrative may unfold.

There is something about the dualism represented by these two edifices that strikes me as profound. To me, they somehow reflect the pattern of the cultural oppression, struggle to gain autonomy, temporary collapse into academic apathy and lethargy, and eventual burst of energetic tribal resurgence that has characterized the last seventy-five years of American Indian education. These two buildings, so close in physical proximity yet so distant in philosophical orientation, are structural symbols, reminders, really, of where we have been and where we appear to be heading.

Sometimes a building can tell stories, if we care to listen.

# Notes

## Introduction

1. It remains a mystery to me why GPS operates in an inconsistent fashion on some reservations. However, on more than one occasion my GPS has directed me to roads that do not exist while navigating through reservation lands. Along with the vagaries of GPS are other technological issues. It is important to note that some reservations also lack cell phone service and convenient Internet service. The issue of Internet service is a particular concern for some reservation schools. A number of reservations, like many other rural locations, must deal with either expensive Internet service, low-speed service, or in some cases no access at all. Unfortunately, disadvantages such as these plague more than a few reservation schools.

2. I have previously referred to reservations as "dichotomous places" because they are the locations of social contradictions (Huffman, 2013, p. 4). Namely, reservations are at once places of cultural and spiritual refuge as well as locations of serious social problems. This duality re-creates much confusion and misunderstanding among those who seek to comprehend the complexities of reservation life.

3. Richard Pratt did not invent boarding schools for American Indian children, but his influence was so great that his name is now almost synonymous with those institutions. Pratt was motivated by what he regarded as a noble humanitarian purpose. Ironically and sadly, Carlisle Indian School, along with many other boarding schools so closely associated with his legacy, frequently inflicted serious harm on Native peoples.

4. Pratt's reference to a "great general" is General Philip Sheridan. When a group of Comanches came to Fort Cobb, Indian Territory (Oklahoma), to surrender, their leader Tosawi (Silver Knife, sometimes also spelled Tosahwi) attempted to placate the general by saying in broken English, "Tosawi, good Indian." Sheridan is reputed to have replied, "The only good Indians I ever saw were dead" (Brown, 1970), thus the origin of the saying, "The only good Indian is a dead Indian." To Pratt's way of thinking, his injunction to "kill the Indian in him and save the man" was a great benevolent alternative to the brutal extermination of the race as suggested in the sentiment expressed by General Sheridan.

5. The facts surrounding this lawsuit constitute its own compelling story complete with intense personal, political, and legal drama. The plaintiffs claimed that the federal government had violated the 1868 Fort Laramie Treaty by allowing "bad men" to come onto the reservation and do harm to the people. However, federal judge Diane Gilbert Sypolt ruled that the plaintiffs did not follow an arcane procedure as outlined in the original treaty regarding the presence and definition of "bad men." Essentially, she ruled that according to the stipulations of the treaty, the plaintiffs were required to

have the Bureau of Indian Affairs adjudicate the case before coming to the courts. In her ruling Judge Sypolt wrote, "Having failed to bring their claims administratively, plaintiffs are barred from seeking relief from the court." Subsequent attempts in South Dakota state courts were also dismissed.

But the story does not end there. In March 2011, when Circuit Court judge Bradley Zell dismissed the case, he also ruled that under South Dakota state law HB 1104 plaintiffs over age forty may collect damages from individual perpetrators of childhood abuse, but they may not collect damages from entities such as the Catholic Church or any religious order that hired and supervised those perpetrators. In effect, the ruling absolved the Catholic Church of any culpability in the sex abuse cases. Additionally, for those over forty, HB 1104 established a time limit of three years to file a civil suit from the time a victim reasonably discovered harm from abuse. Curiously, Judge Zell also ruled that HB 1104 applied to lawsuits filed before its existence. Thus, while the law was not amended until 2010, because of the retroactive nature of the ruling, it applied to the legal actions taken on behalf of American Indians which began in 2003 (Brokaw, 2012; Giago, 2012; Woodard, 2011).

6. Some refute when boarding school enrollments reached their greatest numbers. The debate will likely never be settled as enrollment figures vary greatly and, in the case for many boarding schools, are unreliable. The most accurate estimates of enrollments at boarding schools are found around mid-twentieth century (just before World War II) until the present. Using those figures, the largest enrollments in boarding schools occurred during the termination policy years.

7. It is hard to imagine a man more deeply scorned by his critics, so highly decorated for public service by his superiors, and yet generally unknown by today's public than Dillon S. Myer (1891–1982). Myer began as a professor of agronomy at the University of Kentucky but soon turned to a career in federal public service, a career, it should be noted, that lasted over thirty years and saw Myer serve in major capacities with the Department of Agriculture, the Department of the Interior, the Department of War, and the Department of State. By far his most lasting legacy came as the director of the War Relocation Authority (WRA) from 1942 to 1946 (during which he oversaw the internment of thousands of Japanese Americans in relocation camps) and later as commissioner of Indian Affairs from 1950 to 1953. Both of these appointments led to controversial actions that enshrined Myer among the vilest of racist bureaucrats in American history (Drinnon, 1987). Ironically, President Truman awarded the Medal for Merit to Myer for his efforts leading the WRA. Even more ironic, in 1946 the Japanese American Citizen League praised Myer for his inspiring and courageous leadership. Adding yet another layer of irony, Myer later denounced the relocation program of Japanese Americans as unnecessary and immoral (Myer, 1971). As far as is known, Myer went to his grave unapologetic for the policy of termination. Indeed, he believed sterner measures should have been employed to force more tribes to accept the policy (Myer, 1970).

8. Arthur Watkins (1886–1973) served in the US Senate from 1946 to 1958. During his tenure, Watkins became a major force in American Indian affairs. In 1947 he accepted the chairmanship of the Indian Affairs Subcommittee of the Senate's Committee on Public Lands, a position from which he dominated the hearings on tribal termination until his reelection defeat in 1958. Ironically, Watkins confessed that he reluctantly accepted the chairmanship of the subcommittee (a position in which he could become a permanent fixture in the history of American Indian policy). Years later he recalled that he had accepted the post because "no other Republican would have it" (Grattan-Aiello, 1995, p. 271). However, Larry Haase (1974) disputes Watkins's contention and proposes that he actively sought the chairmanship of the Indian Affairs Subcommittee to help initiate federal American Indian policy change.

Although Watkins earned a reputation for honesty and integrity among his Senate colleagues, historians have closely considered his motivations and actions on American Indian affairs. Watkins was a lifelong and devoted member of the Church of Jesus Christ of Latter-Day Saints (LDS), and by his own admission, this fact influenced his political views and policy positions. While working toward the termination of some tribes, Watkins appeared to give preferential treatment to tribes closely associated with the LDS by curbing efforts to terminate them (Grattan-Aiello, 1995). In a letter written in 1954 to the first presidency of the LDS, Watkins conveyed the intertwining of his political and religious beliefs.

> The more I go into this Indian problem the more I am convinced that we have made some terrible mistakes in the past. It seems to me that the time has come for us to correct some of these mistakes and help the Indians stand on their own two feet and become a white and delightsome people as the Book of Mormon prophesied they would become. Of course, I realize that the Gospel of Jesus Christ will be the motivating factor, but it is difficult to teach the Gospel when they don't understand the English language and have had no training in caring for themselves. The Gospel should be a great stimulus and I am longing and praying for the time when the Indians will accept it in overwhelming numbers. (Grattan-Aiello, 1995, p. 281)

The reference to "white and delightsome" is especially interesting. Traditionally the Church of Jesus Christ of Latter-Day Saints taught that Lamanites (American Indians) would gradually experience a change in skin color upon embracing the *Book of Mormon.* Specifically, 2 Nephi 30:6 reads that "their scales of darkness shall begin to fall from their eyes; and many generations shall not pass away among them, save they shall be a white and a delightsome people." For years this passage was accepted as literal. For instance, in 1960 the president of the LDS remarked that Native children living in Mormon homes through a religious placement program grew to appear lighter in skin tone than Native children remaining on the reservation (Weyler, 1992). In 1981 the word "white" was replaced with the word "pure." Today the LDS interprets this passage as figurative rather than literal.

9. The American Indian Movement was founded in 1968 in Minneapolis, Minnesota. The movement has been cloaked in controversy from its inception to this day. Originally AIM had a decided urban focus, such as monitoring police activity and conduct with Native peoples and offering advocacy for urban American Indians displaced by relocation. However, AIM's attention quickly turned to the social, economic, political, and spiritual issues on reservations. The events at Alcatraz and the Trail of Broken Treaties led to the famous 1973 confrontation at Wounded Knee, South Dakota (the site of the 1890 massacre of Lakota refugees). The resulting siege at Wounded Knee had the planned effect of drawing public attention to the plight of American Indians and to failed federal Indian policies. Nevertheless, taken together, the events at Alcatraz, the Trail of Broken Treaties, and especially the seventy-one-day siege at Wounded Knee solidified AIM's reputation as a militant organization in the eyes of many public officials, private citizens, and, ironically, individual American Indians (Smith & Warrior, 1996).

10. Many scholars have aggressively attacked the culture of poverty thesis for what they consider its blaming-the-victim logic. Such scholars as Edwin Eames and Judith Goode (1973) and Michael Katz (1986, 1989) argue that the culture of poverty thesis tends to pathologize the poor based on privileged middle-class values and fails to fully appreciate the cumulative historical processes and prevailing socioeconomic structures that generate as well as maintain persistent poverty.

11. The argument essentially means that it is easier to blame forces outside the school and beyond the control of educators for the lack of academic success than to exert the necessary effort within the school to ensure greater school success for poor and minority students (Erickson, 1987).

12. Much of this criticism surrounds a lack of comprehension of the complex nature of traditional Lakota values and behavioral expectations, such as those related to humility (Deloria, 1969). Additionally, Wax appeared to completely disregard the four cardinal Lakota virtues—courage, fortitude, generosity, and wisdom—and their importance to both personal conduct and community expectations (Hassrick, 1964).

## 1. Voices from the Reservation Classroom

1. *Wakanyeja* is the Lakota word for children. Based on my conversations with Lakota individuals, especially more tribally traditional people, it is widely regarded as one of the most powerful concepts in the Lakota language, as children are thought to be imbued with unique spiritual qualities generally lost among adults. "Wakanyeja" literally means "scared beings."
2. It is unclear when Sitting Bull uttered these famous words. In all likelihood he made this statement and similar comments on several occasions. What is known, however, is that Sitting Bull visited the small school at Fort Yates located on the Standing Rock reservation shortly before his murder. It is likely that he made a statement similar to the one attributed to him here, as he was prone to promote the benefits of formal education to his people by this time of his life (Vestal, 1934).
3. It is not my contention that inner-city communities are devoid of all hope and that hopefulness is universally found on reservations. Quite the contrary, many who work and sacrifice in our inner cities are driven by an overpowering hope for the future. Likewise, the high rates of suicide and substance abuse, most notably alcoholism, stand as stark reminders of the hopelessness many reservation residents feel. With that said, I do find that reservation educators display a ubiquitous hopefulness that I honestly cannot say I hear pervasively among educators in inner-city schools. I personally believe the difference is that many Native people, especially Native educators, can look to the promise of tribal cultural revitalization that can restore identity and dignity in ways that inner-city peoples do not have available to them at this moment.
4. Technically, this aspect of my research would be considered a case study of six American Indian educators. As such, the research methodology, including sampling strategy, triangulation of data sources, analytic procedures, and creating profiles of the individual cases are all consistent with this social scientific research approach (see, for instance, Yin, 2014). However, I elected to specifically not discuss the methodological technicalities and details. My desire is to focus on the humanity of the participants rather than risk the book sounding too much like a formal, scholarly monograph. I accept any criticism related to that decision.

## 2. Tribal Strengths and American Indian Educators

1. It was a beautiful early fall day, and the children clearly enjoyed their recess. There was subdued laughter and chatter, and I was still struck by how generally quiet the children played. Later I asked about the nature of the recess and was told that was typical for the school and had been for as long as anyone could remember.
2. From my previous visits I already knew that it had been many years since the school had a male teacher. But on this day the teachers were curious as to how the students would respond to me in a "teacher-like role." With the wonderful humor the Lakota are famous for, I was informed I might make a "passable" second grade teacher.
3. The authors refer to their methodology as the Wildfire Research Method first introduced by Janie Hodson (2004). Not only did the six participants engage in a talking circle facilitated by an elder and a researcher over a three-day period, but the retreat was also conducted at a location that "had symbolic and spiritual significance" (Kitchen et

al., 2009, p. 360). Moreover, the approach invited "participants to share their experiences and observations in a Talking Circle, provided a communal and sacred research environment respectful of the traditions and cultural beliefs of Aboriginal people and the importance of a relationship with the land" (p. 360).

4. The perception that Native educators are undervalued is consistent with the findings from the parent study to the research reported in this book (see Huffman, 2013). I found that one-third of the twenty-one American Indian educators I interviewed believed Native educators are not as highly regarded as non-Native educators. Most notable in this regard is the perceived lack of respect afforded by those in upper administration and on school boards.

5. The contention that educators serving in reservation schools encounter multiple perplexing challenges is also consistent with the findings reported in the larger study with the twenty-one Native educators (Huffman, 2013). I too found that the educators were confronted by a collection of issues I coded under the general theme of "reservation social conditions." Most prevalent and vexing among these conditions were pervasive poverty, substance abuse, and family dysfunctions.

6. The finding reported by Kitchen et al. (2009) that the Native educators feel compelled to establish their cultural legitimacy before their communities is supported by June Beynon's (2008) research. She too reported First Nations educators experienced similar dilemmas. While both Kitchen et al. and Beynon found that Native educators feel pressure to institute their tribal identities within their own communities, the twenty-one educators I interviewed did not seem to experience this quandary (Huffman, 2013). Many felt stress from what they considered community scrutiny (specifically, the perception that they needed to not make any missteps because the community was closely watching them), but generally they regarded their ethnicity as their most valuable resource. That is, they believed that the fact they were Native educators from the reservation created greater legitimacy in the estimation of parents and students.

7. In the parent study with twenty-one educators, I found they generally identified serving as a role model as a necessary part of being an American Indian educator in reservation schools (Huffman, 2013). Indeed, it is the pervasiveness of this responsibility that served to identity the type of educator I refer to as "affinitive educators." That is, affinitive educators specifically believed their primary obligation was to be a role model for their students. Moreover, among the twenty-one individuals, affinitive educators (twelve) outnumbered the individuals I identified as "facilitative educators" (nine). Not surprisingly, this theme emerged once again when interviewing the six individuals included in the case study reported here.

8. I refer to Donna Deyhle's work as "classic" for several reasons. First, I believe her findings are among the most powerful and thoroughly nuanced insights found in the literature. In many respects Deyhle broke ground and established a research trail for others to follow. Second, her research is classic in the sense of the pervasiveness to which other scholars reference her work. Indeed it is difficult to find a study on American Indian high school persistence/attrition that still does not reference Deyhle's study of high school leavers. The quality of the work has simply stood the test of time.

9. The Lakota Flag Song is at times referred to the Lakota National Anthem. The singing of the Flag Song is a highly regarded ceremony among the Lakota. It pays honor to those you have served in the armed forces and recognizes the Lakota nation's commitment to defend the United States. Translated into English, the lyrics in part say, "The President's flag will stand forever and under it the people live, therefore I do this." The Lakota, like many other tribal nations, have the highest percentage of veterans in the United States. Respect for veterans is a highly significant tribal value.

10. Like so many other aspects of this enigmatic historical figure's life, the events surrounding Crazy Horse's death and his final deathbed speech are shrouded in mystery and

disagreement (Josephy, 1974; Powers, 2010; Sandoz, 1942). A number of contradictory accounts of his death persist. What is certain is that he succumbed to a mortal stab wound to the back in all likelihood inflicted by a soldier's bayonet. Although in excruciating pain, ever defiant to the end, he refused to lay in a white man's cot and insisted on being placed on the floor. After lingering for hours in dreadful agony, Crazy Horse died of peritonitis (Bray, 2006; Powers, 2010). Even those to whom Crazy Horse confided his final speech is open to debate. Some contend he made his address to Lieutenant Colonel Luther Prentice Bradley, the post commander at Fort Robinson. This seems highly unlikely as Bradley deliberately avoided the dying Crazy Horse (Bray, 2006; Marshall, 2004). It is more probable that Crazy Horse spoke to the post surgeon, Dr. Valentine McGillycuddy, who attended him up until his final moments, and Lieutenant Jesse Lee, the agent of the Spotted Tail Agency who was also in the room when he died (McGillycuddy, 1929). The deathbed speech, which has been published numerous times, is honest, elegant, and dignified.

### 3. Tribal Strengths and American Indian Students

1. Tammy and I agreed to conduct this exercise before I visited her class. It came soon after Montana's American Indian Heritage Day (the fourth Friday of September), and the students had been considering the nature of their ethnicity, tribal history, and shared history with all tribal nations. This may partially account for the general seriousness of answers to my question. However, more likely it simply suggests that they took the question seriously. On a related note, I tried the same exercise with a class of second graders on a South Dakota reservation. I didn't get quite the same results. The students generally just looked at me and giggled. But I did get one unforgettable response from a seven-year-old boy who looked at me very seriously and proclaimed, "My cousin is a real Indian!"

2. That particular research project was a five-year study frequently involving multiple interviews with American Indian students attending a predominately non-Indian college. The results revealed deeply nuanced insights on the college experience, including factors associated with retention and attrition of Native college students. Most notable of all, however, is the importance of a person's ethnic identity to the college experience. I reported the findings of the research in a book entitled *American Indian Higher Educational Experiences: Cultural Visions and Personal Journeys* (2008). The story of the lost girl and the eagle as recounted by the student is also found in *American Indian Higher Educational Experiences.*

3. "Acting white" is a controversial concept, and not everyone agrees to its pervasiveness. Generally, the notion is that African American youth (and perhaps other minority youths) can be subjected to severe criticism from their peers if they are academically successful. In essence, an accusation of acting white condemns the person for "selling out" his/her race and accepting the expectations (especially those related to academic success) of white society (Buck, 2010; Fryer, 2006; Ogbu, 2003).

4. Students of sociological theory will recognize that this is essentially the same conclusion reached by Émile Durkheim in his famous study on suicide rates in Europe at the end of the nineteenth century (Durkheim, Spaulding, & Simpson, 1966). For Durkheim, anomic suicide occurs when individuals feel lost and alone as social values and cohesion breakdown. Experts frequently identify teenage suicide as an example of this form of suicide (Abrutyn & Mueller, 2014; Phillips, 2014).

5. Flandreau Indian School (FIS) is only one of four remaining Bureau of Indian Education–sponsored boarding schools. The other three include Chemawa Indian School in Salem, Oregon; Riverside Indian School in Anadarko, Oklahoma; and Sherman Indian High School in Riverside, California. Flandreau Indian School has an

interesting and usual history. The town of Flandreau, South Dakota, was founded by a group of Santee Dakota homesteading along the Big Sioux River in 1869. They petitioned the federal government for a school in order to avoid being forced to send their children to distant boarding schools. The petition was granted, and FIS was founded in 1891 and has been in continuous service since (Lee, 2013).

6. In one of the most widely recognized ethnographies of the Lakota, *The Sioux: Life and Customs of a Warrior Society* (University of Oklahoma Press, 1964), Royal Hassrick described the tiyospaye: "The *tiyospe*, a group of individuals banded together under a common leader and often related through descent or marriage to the patriarch, was the ancient and important core of Sioux society. Through the able guidance of an experienced and dependable elder, small groups of people co-operated in hunting and in war; in carrying out the daily chores of homemaking, rearing children, celebrating, and worshipping; in caring for the aged; and in burying the dead. To accomplish all of these successfully, the *tiyospe* was of necessity an intensely cohesive organization. In general, the *tiyospe* was composed of members of one or more families, and because of interrelation of family members was subject to a patterned system, the *tiyospe* itself was imbued with a sense of order" (p. 97).

## 4. Tribal Strengths and the Craft of Teaching

1. Chief Dan George (1899–1981) was, true to his name, an actual chief of the Tsleil-Waututh Nation located along the coast of British Columbia. Although George did not begin acting until he was 60 years old, he quickly gained notoriety during the 1960s and 1970s playing American Indian roles in a number of major motion pictures as well as a variety of television productions. George stole the show in *Little Big Man* (1970) playing the role of Old Lodge Skins (for which he was nominated for an Academy Award for best supporting actor) opposite Dustin Hoffman; then he stole it again playing the role of Old Watie in *The Outlaw Josey Wales* (1976) starring Clint Eastwood. Chief Dan George used his late-in-life celebrity well. He strived to promote the rights and integrity of First Nations peoples. In 1967 he delivered a powerful soliloquy, *Lament for Confederation*, in Vancouver as part of the Canadian centennial celebration. Many scholars and political leaders regard this monologue as playing an important role in initiating First Nations political activism while simultaneously gaining support among many in the non–First Nations population (Armstrong, 2005). So beloved is Chief Dan George that in 2008 the Canadian government issued a postage stamp in his honor.

2. Along with Tammy, Ben, Donna, and Rachel also described encounters with racism from teachers and administrators while they were students in reservation schools.

3. Educators generally accept the premise and assumptions behind culturally relevant educational approaches. However, even Geneva Gay (2002), one of the most ardent proponents of culturally relevant education, acknowledges that this acceptance is hardly universal. Some question the logic and methods associated with culturally relevant education. Most notable, they challenge the notion that an individual student's abilities should somehow be associated with allegedly group attributes (Gay, 2010; Fasching-Varner & Dodo-Seriki, 2012). Thus, according to this criticism, culturally relevant educational approaches can engender its own form of stereotyping minority students.

4. What I refer to here as culturally relevant education is similar to culture-based education (CBE) frequently found in the American Indian education literature (Demmert, 2011; Mohatt, Trimble, & Dickson, 2006; Powers, Potthoff, Bearinger, & Resnick, 2003). Culture-based education is closely associated with a specific theoretical perspective generally referred to as "cultural discontinuity theory." This theory asserts that a cultural incongruence between the values and behavioral expectations found in American Indian homes and mainstream schools places Native students at a decided

academic disadvantage (Huffman, 2010). As Mohatt et al. explain, "The guiding assumption of CBE is that a discontinuity between home and school environments serves to confuse and alienate indigenous children, fostering a sense of inadequacy and lack of self-efficacy. Factors implicated in this discontinuity include value differences between home and school, social organization, the absence of accurate statements about American Indian / Alaska Native cultures by teachers and in textbooks, and differences in language" (2006, p. 39). The major difference in terms is that my use of culturally relevant education is intended to be more sweeping and includes a range of educational pedagogical practices and is not necessarily associated with the premise and assumptions of cultural discontinuity theory.

5. Indian Education for All is a Montana State initiative designed to infuse the history and culture of the state's Native tribes across the curriculum for all grade levels and for all students, both Native and non-Native. It is an ambitious effort. As Lynn Kelting-Gibson describes it, "Despite a vast array of research and primary sources that provide a complex and highly textured history, a simplistic version of how non-Indians settled the North American continent persists in most classrooms around the nation. Montana's Indian Education for All (IEFA) Act offers a remarkable opportunity to change that. The law requires that all of Montana's children learn the history and culture of the 12 tribes and seven reservations spread across the state" (2006, p. 204).

6. As of this writing, the status of No Child Left Behind as an education policy is at best murky. The policy officially remains in effect, although an individual state may request a waiver relieving it from NCLB mandates. Yet, a state is not completely free of the policy's essential premise, as a waiver request requires the state to outline its own standards-based requirements (and presumably sanctions for failing to meet standards). The heavy-handed sanctions of the first ten years of NCLB have largely disappeared, yet sanctions can still be imposed under specific conditions. It is a baffling arrangement that has opened the door to such supposed corrective (albeit just as controversial) measures as Race to the Top and Common Core (McDonnell & Weatherford, 2013).

7. The proficiency assessments of American Indian students under the present standards and testing procedures are frustrating to teachers, administrators, parents, and students (Morris, Pae, Arrington, & Sevick, 2006). Many scholars and practitioners argue that current assessment tools and strategies are woefully inadequate to measure the true academic proficiencies of Native children and youth (Demmert, 2005; Huffman, 2013; Lomawaima & McCarty, 2006).

8. Rachel's second-graders were having difficulty keeping still and displaying the required respect by being quiet during the singing of the Flag Song (not surprising for seven-year-olds). She took the opportunity not only to correct inappropriate behavior but also to deliver an important lesson on traditional Lakota values and expectations.

9. Smudging is a common purification ceremony among tribal and nontribal peoples throughout the world. As I briefly mentioned in chapter 1, as practiced by the Lakota, smudging typically involves the burning of either sweet grass (to encourage the influence of good spirits) or sage grass (to discourage and ward away evil spirits). The person fans the smoke into one's face and body while praying as a means of purification. The smoke then carries the prayers to the Creator.

10. In many respects, this is an odd statement to make. Although individual Native people may reject any and all forms of spirituality, all American Indian nations, historically and contemporarily, are spiritual owing to the social fact that their cultures are inseparable from spirituality (Hassrick, 1964). For many Native persons, it is simply impossible to compartmentalize one's spirituality from his/her identity and being. When Tim Giago, the award-winning editor and founder of *Indian Country Today* and a Harvard University Nieman Fellow, was asked to discuss the influence of Lakota spirituality on his work as a journalist, he explained the impossibility of adequately answering such a question.

In Lakota the word "wakan" means many things. It means a spirituality that is either received or transmitted. Wakan means that which is hard to understand because it is filled with such mystery. It means that spirituality is within us, all around us, or sent to us through a vision or through the love and passion of another. These things are all a part and parcel of that great mystery we call our spirituality. The Lakota and the other Indian tribes of the Western Hemisphere did not have what could be called a religion. Religion is something that is organized, dogmatic and based on the written word. The Bible and Koran, for instance, are written documents that define the parameters to which the faithful in these religions must adhere in order to be saved and served. Instead, Indian tribes had a spiritual connection with the earth, wind, sky, water, fire, sun, moon, birds, fish and those animals that walked upon four legs . . . When one understands that an Indian's spirituality begins with the morning sun and is then a part of every motion and moment all of that day and night—then one perceives there is no separation between the physical, mental or spiritual being. It is all one all of the time. Even for an Indian journalist. (1997, p. 41)

## 5. Tribal Strengths and Reservation Schools

1. Actually, there are at least five established theoretical perspectives generally used by American Indian education scholars: cultural discontinuity theory; structural inequality theory; critical race theory; transculturation theory; and interactionalist theory (also referred to as institutional departure theory). Interactionalist theory was introduced by Vincent Tinto (1987, 1988) and has since become an enormously popular perspective among scholars interested in higher educational persistence and departure (Braxton, 2002). While the theory itself was not originally designed to specially address the nature of higher education persistence/attrition for minorities per se, it still has been used as a framework to account for college attrition among many minority groups, including American Indians (Belgarde & Loré, 2003; Huffman, 2003; Murguiá, Padilla, & Pavel, 1991; Taylor, 2005). As is the case with any popular theoretical framework, it has also gained a great deal of criticism. Most notably, critics charge that because interactionalist theory developed as a means to explain white, middle-class collegiate experiences, it inadequately accounts for the unique experiences of poor or minority students (Pidgeon, 2008; Rendon, Jalomo, & Nora, 2002; Tierney, 1992). I have elected not to discuss interactionalist theory in this treatment because the perspective is specifically designed to explain general higher educational persistence and attrition. Moreover, scholars do not typically use this framework to examine and explain the educational experience of Native students enrolled in reservation elementary and secondary schools. A fuller consideration of Tinto's interactionalist theory is found in *Theoretical Perspectives on American Indian Education* (Huffman, 2010).

2. Social inequality theory owes a great deal to the seminal work of educational anthropologist John Ogbu (1939–2003). Especially influential is Ogbu's cultural-ecological theory, which attempts to account for why some minority group members flourish academically while other minority group members tend to fare poorly. Essentially, Ogbu (1978, 1987, 1991, 1992, 2003) argued that there are three types of minorities in the United States: autonomous minorities, voluntary minorities, and involuntary minorities. Each type has unique historical circumstances and experiences with the mainstream society. As a result, each type of minority has developed specific responses and attitudes toward mainstream education. Namely, autonomous and voluntary minorities tend to regard mainstream education as a means for upward mobility and generally thrive academically. Unfortunately, involuntary minorities (such as American Indians) have experienced hostile and negative encounters with the greater society and the institution of education in particular. Involuntary minorities tend to regard schools as foreign institutions imposed on them for the benefit of white society. As such, they adopt antagonistic dispositions toward education and frequently have difficulty

perceiving the personal benefit of an educational system they see as arranged for the advantage of the dominant race.

3. The notion of personal and social "color blindness" raises serious concerns among many people. While some believe that color blindness in personal relationships leads to harmony and respect as it supposedly makes no distinction between individuals, others contend such a claim of racial objectivity is a potentially dangerous conception as it can lead people to ignore significant social inequities. In its extreme forms, assertions of color blindness can be used as a rationalization for discounting persistent and real social inequities in society. Eduardo Bonilla-Silva (2006) calls this kind of color blindness the "new racism." In scathing criticism, he relates:

> Yet this new ideology has become a formidable political tool for the maintenance of the racial order. Much as Jim Crow racism served as the glue for defending a brutal and overt system of racial oppression in the pre-Civil Rights era, color-blind racism serves today as the ideological armor for a covert and institutionalized system in the post-Civil Rights era. And the beauty of this new ideology is that it aids in the maintenance of white privilege without fanfare, without naming those who it rewards . . . Shielded by color-blindness, whites can express resentment toward minorities; criticize their morality, values, and work ethic; and even claim to be victim of reverse racism. (pp. 3–4)

4. The other theoretical perspectives discussed in this chapter grew out of more general treatments of minority education and were subsequently applied by scholars of American Indian education. Even tribal critical race theory originally developed from the larger field of critical race theory, which actually developed out of an even larger field—critical studies (Delgado & Stefancic, 2001; Lindley, 2009).

5. In her research examining the educational experiences of the eight American Indian college students, White Shield (2009) also introduced a novel research technique she refers to as the Medicine Wheel Culturally Intrinsic Research Paradigm. The approach calls for collaborating with tribal elders in interpreting the findings of a research endeavor. Specifically, the researcher integrates the perspectives and wisdom of tribal elders into the analysis of the findings in order to gain a deeper understanding and appreciation of their significance.

6. Obviously, one must be careful not to stereotype individuals according to presumed values, attitudes, and behaviors. Such simplistic characterizations are unfair and doomed for inaccuracy. Nevertheless, previous research provides evidence of a pronounced pattern for culturally oriented American Indian college students to display a desire for community service in their projected careers paths more persistently than non-Native college students or even Native students who are not as culturally oriented (Huffman, 2008, 2011; Lee, 2009; Pavel, Banks, & Pavel, 2002; Zahrt, 2001).

7. Interestingly, Donna, Rachel, and Lori were all Lakota from South Dakota. They came from a reservation that is generally regarded as culturally traditional. From my experience and perspective, spiritual expressions of their tribal culture are more common and expected than in the communities of the three Montana educators.

8. The school building described in this chapter is not located on any of the reservation residences of the six participants in this study. In fact, this school is not even in Montana or South Dakota. The building is falling into a dilapidated condition due in part to its nebulous legal standing. Although originally built by the Bureau of Indian Affairs, it passed into ownership of the state's regional school district, which operated the reservation's school system via a memo of understanding. The tribal government is considering buying the building and adjacent buildings for reservation use owing to its current status as non-used surplus property. As I understand the situation, the discussion over the purchase and use of the property has sparked considerable debate among the local reservation population generated in large part over the emotions elicited by what the building represents.

# References

Abrutyn, S., & Mueller, A. (2014). The socioemotional foundations of suicide. *Sociological Theory, 32*(4), 327–51.

Adams, D. W. (1995). *Education for extinction: American Indians and the boarding school experience, 1875–1928.* Lawrence, KS: University Press of Kansas.

Almeida, D. A. (1996). *Countering prejudice against American Indians and Alaska Natives through antibias curriculum and instruction.* Clearinghouse on Rural Education and Small Schools (EDO-RC-96-4). Charleston, WV: Appalachia Educational Laboratory.

Almeida, D. A. (1998). Indigenous education: Survival for our children. *Equity and Excellence in Education, 31*(1), 6–10.

Amerman, S. (2007). "I should not be wearing a Pilgrim hat": Making an Indian place in urban schools, 1945–1975. *American Indian Culture and Research Journal, 31*(1), 39–62.

Aragon, S. R. (2002). An investigation of factors influencing classroom motivation for postsecondary American Indian / Alaska Native students. *Journal of American Indian Education, 41*(1), 1–18.

Archuleta, M. L., Child, B. J., & Lomawaima, K. T. (2000). *Away from home: American Indian boarding school experiences, 1879–2000.* Phoenix, AZ: Heard Museum.

Armstrong, C. (2005). Profile of Chief Dan George. In D. Newhouse, C. Voyageur, & D. Beavon (Eds.), *Hidden in plain sight: Contributions of Aboriginal peoples to Canadian identity and culture* (pp. 14–18). Toronto, ON: University of Toronto Press.

Au, K. H. (1993). *Literacy instruction in multicultural settings.* Fort Worth, TX: Harcourt Brace Jovanovich.

Banfield, E. (1977). *The unheavenly city revisited.* Boston: Little, Brown.

Barnhardt, R., & Kawagley, A. O. (2005). Indigenous knowledge systems and Native Alaska ways of knowing. *Anthropology & Education Quarterly, 36*(1), 8–23.

Begaye, T. (2007). Native teacher understanding of culture as a concept for curricular inclusion. *Wicazo Sa Review, 22*(1), 35–52.

Belgarde, M. J., & Loré, R. K. (2003). The retention/intervention of Native American undergraduates at the University of New Mexico. *Journal of College Student Retention, 52*(2), 175–202.

Bell, L., & Marlow, P. E. (2009). Visibility, healing and resistance: Voices from the 2005 Dena'ina Language Institute. *Journal of American Indian Education, 48*(1), 1–18.

Bennett, T. (2011). Culture, choice, necessity: A political critique of Bourdieu's aesthetic. *Poetics, 39*(6), 530–46.

Berry, B. (1968). *The education of the American Indian: A survey of the literature.* Washington, DC: US Department of Health, Education, and Welfare, Bureau of Research.

Beynon, J. (2008). *First Nations teachers: Identity and community, struggle and change.* Calgary, AB: Detselig.

Biber, B. (1967). *Young deprived children and their educational needs.* Washington, DC: Association for Childhood International.

Bloom, B. S., Davis, A., & Hess, R. D. (1965). *Contemporary education for cultural deprivation.* New York: Holt, Rinehart and Winston.

Bomer, R., Dworin, J. E., May, L., & Semingson, P. (2008). Miseducating teachers about the poor: A critical analysis of Ruby Payne's claims about poverty. *Teachers College Record, 110*(12), 2497–2531.

Bonilla-Silva, E. (2006). *Racism without racists: Color-blind racism and the persistence of racial inequality in the United States.* Lanham, MD: Rowman & Littlefield.

Bourdieu, P. (1977). *Reproduction in education, society, culture.* Beverly Hills, CA: Sage.

Bourdieu, P. (1986). The forms of capital. In J. G. Richardson (Ed.), *Handbook of theory and research in the sociology of education* (pp. 241–58). Westport, CT: Greenwood.

Bourdieu, P., & Passeron, J. C. (1990). *Reproduction in education, society, and culture.* London, UK: Sage.

Boyer, P. (2006). It takes a Native community: Educators reform schools in an era of standards. *Tribal College Journal, 17*(4), 13–19.

Braxton, J. M. (2002). Introduction: Reworking the student departure puzzle. In J. M. Braxton (Ed.), *Reworking the student departure puzzle* (pp. 1–8). Nashville, TN: Vanderbilt University Press.

Bray, K. M. (2006). *Crazy Horse: A Lakota life.* Norman, OK: University of Oklahoma Press.

Brayboy, B. (2005). Toward a tribal critical race theory in education. *Urban Review, 37*(5), 425–46.

Brokaw, C. (2012, September 7). SD court upholds dismissal of school abuse lawsuit. *Native Times.* Retrieved from http://www.nativetimes.com /new/crime.

Brown, D. (1970). *Bury my heart at Wounded Knee*. New York: Holt, Rinehart, and Winston.

Bryde, J. (1971). *Modern Indian psychology*. Vermillion, SD: Institute of Indian Studies, University of South Dakota.

Buck, S. (2010). *Acting White: The ironic legacy of desegregation*. New Haven, CT: Yale University Press.

Cajete, G. (2006). It is time for Indian people to define Indigenous education on our own terms. *Tribal College Journal, 18*(2), 56–57.

Carney, C. M. (1999). *Native American higher education in the United States*. New Brunswick, NJ: Transaction.

Chadwick, B. A. (1972). The inedible feast. In H. M. Bahr, B. A. Chadwick, & R. C. Day (Eds.), *Native Americans today: Sociological perspectives* (pp. 131–45). New York: Harper and Row.

Chafel, J. A. (1997). Societal images of poverty. *Youth and Society, 28*(June), 432–63.

Chandler, P. T. (2011). Critical race theory and social studies: Centering the Native American experience. *Journal of Social Science Research, 34*(1), 29–58.

Chandler, P. T., & McKnight, D. (2008). Social studies and the social order: Telling stories of resistance. *Teacher Education Quarterly, 36*(1), 59–75.

Cheeseman, G. W., & Gapp, S. C. (2012). Integrating storytelling into the mindset of prospective teachers of American Indian students: A grounded theory. *Multicultural Education, 19*(4), 24–32.

Cherubini, L. (2008). New Aboriginal teachers' experiences: An undiscovered landscape. *Canadian Journal of Native Education, 31*(2), 34–50.

Cherubini, L., Kitchen, J., & Trudeau, L. (2009). Having the spirit within to vision: New Aboriginal teachers' commitment to reclaiming space. *Canadian Journal of Native Education, 32*(2), 38–51.

Cherubini, L., Niemczyk, E., Hodson, J., & McGean, S. (2010). A grounded theory of new Aboriginal teachers' perceptions: The cultural attributions of Medicine Wheel teachings. *Teachers and Teaching: Theory and Practice, 16*(5), 545–57.

Child, Brenda J. (1998). *Boarding school seasons: American Indian families, 1900–1940*. Lincoln, NE: University of Nebraska Press.

Cleary, L. M., & Peacock, T. (1998). *Collected wisdom: American Indian education*. Needham Heights, NJ: Allyn and Bacon.

Coladarci, T. (1983). High-school dropouts among Native Americans. *Journal of American Indian Education, 23*(1), 15–22.

Colmant, S., Schultz, L., Robbins, R., Ciali, P., Dorton, J., & Rivera-Colmant, Y. (2004). Constructing meaning to the Indian boarding school experience. *Journal of American Indian Education, 43*(3), 22–40.

Cornell, S., & Kalt, J. P. (2010). *American Indian self-determination: Political economy of a policy that works* (RWP 10–043). Cambridge, MA: Kennedy School of Government.

Crenshaw, K., Gotanda, N., Peller, G., & Thomas, K. (1995). *Critical race theory: The key writings that formed the movement.* New York: New Press.

Crow, L., Murray, W., & Smythe, H. (1966). *Educating the culturally disadvantaged child: Principles and programs.* New York: David McKay Company.

Cueva, B. M. (2013). Theorizing the racial and gendered educational experiences of Chicanas and Native American women in Ph.D. level in higher education: Testimonies of resistance, defiance, survival, and hope. Doctoral dissertation, UCLA, Los Angeles, CA.

Cummings, J. (1992). The empowerment of Indian students. In J. Reyhner (Ed.), *Teaching American Indian students* (pp. 3–12). Norman, OK: University of Oklahoma Press.

Davis, J. (1992). Factors contributing to post-secondary achievement of American Indians. *Tribal College Journal, 4*(2), 24–30.

Delgado, R., & Stefancic, J. (2001). *Critical race theory: An introduction.* New York: New York University Press.

Deloria, V. (1969). *Custer died for your sins.* New York: Avon.

Deloria, V., & Wildcat, D. (2001). *Power and place: Indian education in America.* Boulder, CO: Fulcrum Resources.

DeMillie, R. J. (2009). Community in Native America: Continuity and change among the Sioux. *Journal de la Société des Américanistes, 95*(1), 185–205.

Demmert, W. G. (2005). The influences of culture on learning and assessment among Native American Indians. *Learning Disabilities Research & Practice, 20*(1), 16–23.

Demmert, W. G. (2011). What is culture-based education? Understanding pedagogy and curriculum. In J. Reyhner, W. S. Gilbert, & L. Lockard (Eds.), *Honoring our heritage: Culturally appropriate approaches for teaching Indigenous students* (pp. 1–9). Flagstaff, AZ: Northern Arizona University Press.

Deyhle, D. (1994). Constructing failure and maintaining cultural identity. *Journal of American Indian Education, 31*(2), 24–47.

Deyhle, D., & LeCompte, M. (1994). Cultural differences in child development: Navajo adolescents in middle school. *Theory into Practice, 33,* 156–78.

Di Silvestro, R. (2005). *In the shadow of Wounded Knee: The untold final story of the Indian Wars.* New York: Walker and Company.

Drinnon, R. (1987). *Keeper of concentration camps: Dillon S. Myer and American racism.* Berkeley, CA: University of California Press.

Duquette, C. (2002). Becoming a teacher: Expectations of First Nations student teachers in isolated communities. *Canadian Journal of Native Education, 24*(2), 134–43.

Durkheim, E., Spaulding, J. A., & Simpson, G. (1966). *Suicide : A study in sociology.* New York: Free Press.

Eames, E., & Goode, J. G. (1973). *Urban poverty in a cross-cultural context.* New York: Free Press.

Erickson, F. (1987). Transformation and school success: The politics and culture of educational attainment. *Anthropology & Education Quarterly, 18*(4), 335–56.

Erickson, J. L., Terhune, M. N., & Ruff, W. G. (2008). Measuring work conditions for teachers of American Indian students. *Researcher, 21*(2), 1–10.

Erikson, E. H. (1950). *Childhood and society.* New York: Norton.

Erikson, E. H. (1963). *Childhood and society.* New York: Norton.

Erikson, E. H. (1968). *Identity: Youth and crisis.* New York: Norton.

Erikson, E. H. (1980). *Identity and the life cycle.* New York: Norton.

Falk, D., & Aitken, L. (1984). Promoting retention among American Indian college students. *Journal of American Indian Education, 23*(2), 24–31.

Fasching-Varner, K., & Dodo-Seriki, V. (2012). Moving beyond seeing with our eyes wide shut: A response to "There is no culturally responsive teaching spoken here." *Democracy and Education, 20*(1), 1–6.

Fenimore-Smith, J. K. (2009). The power of place: Creating an Indigenous charter school. *Journal of American Indian Education, 48*(2), 1–17.

Fixico, D. L. (1986). *Termination and relocation: Federal Indian policy, 1945–1960.* Albuquerque, NM: University of New Mexico Press.

Fixico, D. L. (2000). *The urban Indian experience in America.* Albuquerque, NM: University of New Mexico Press.

Fleming, W. C. (2006). Myths and stereotypes about Native Americans. *Phi Delta Kappan, 88*(3), 213–16.

Fletcher, M. (2008). *American Indian education: Counternarratives in racism, struggle, and the law.* New York: Routledge.

Forbes, J. (2000). The new assimilation movement: Standards, tests, and Anglo-American supremacy. *Journal of American Indian Education, 39*(2), 7–28.

Fordham, M. (1998). The politics of language and the survival of Indigenous culture: From suppression to reintroduction in the formal classroom. *Equity and Excellence in Education, 31*(1), 40–47.

Freedman, E. (2011, June). Bay Mills' bold approach: Public school academies preserve native culture and language with commitment to increasing student achievement. *Diverse,* 18–19.

French, S. E., Seidman, E., Allen, L., & Aber, J. L. (2006). The development of ethnic identity during adolescence. *Developmental Psychology, 42*(1), 1–10.

Friesen, D. W., & Orr, J. (1998). New paths, old ways: Exploring the places of influence on the role identity. *Canadian Journal of Native Education, 22*(2), 188–200.

Fryer, R. G. (2006). "Acting white": The social price paid by the best and brightest minority students. *Education Next, 6*(1), 53–59.

Fuller, A. (2012, August). In the shadow of Wounded Knee. *National Geographic, 222*(2), 30–67.

Gans, H. (1995). *The war against the poor: The underclass and antipoverty policy.* New York: Basic Books.

Garoutte, E., Goldberg, J., Beals, J., Herrell, R., Manson, S., & AI-SUPERPFP Team. (2003). Spirituality and attempted suicide among American Indians. *Social Science and Medicine, 56,* 1571–79.

Garrett, M. (1995). Between two worlds: Cultural discontinuity in the dropout of Native American youth. *School Counselor, 42*(3), 186–95.

Garrett, M., Bellon-Harn, M., Torres-Rivera, E., Garrett, J., & Roberts, L. (2003). Open hands, open hearts: Working with Native youth in the schools. *Intervention in School and Clinic, 38*(4), 225–35.

Gay, G. (2002). Preparing for culturally responsive teaching. *Journal of Teacher Education, 53*(2), 106–16.

Gay, G. (2010). *Culturally responsive teaching* (2nd ed.). New York: Teachers College Press.

Giago, T. (1997). American Indian spirituality. *Nieman Reports, 51*(3), 41.

Giago, T. (2012, February 19). Addressing the most discriminatory bill ever passed in South Dakota. *Native Times.* Retrieved from http://www.nativetimes.com/life/commentary.

Gorski, P. C. (2008). Peddling poverty for profit: Elements of oppression in Ruby Payne's framework. *Equity and Excellence in Education, 41*(1), 130–48.

Grande, S. (2004). *Red pedagogy: Native American social and political thought.* Lanham, MD: Rowman & Littlefield.

Grattan-Aiello, C. (1995). Senator Arthur V. Watkins and the termination of Utah's Southern Paiute Indians. *Utah Historical Quarterly, 63*(3), 268–83.

Gregory, G. A. (2013). Principles of indigenous education for mainstream teaching. In J. Reyhner, J. Martin, L. Lockard, & W. S. Gilbert (Eds.), *Honoring our children: Culturally appropriate approaches for teaching indigenous children.* Flagstaff, AZ: Northern Arizona University Press.

Guild, P. (1994). The culture/learning style connection. *Educational Leadership, 51*(1), 16–21.

Guillory, J. (1993). *Cultural capital: The problem of literary canon formation.* Chicago, IL: University of Chicago Press.

Haase, L. (1974). Termination and assimilation: Federal Indian policy, 1943–1961. Doctoral dissertation, Washington State University, Pullman, WA.

Hardy, S. A., & Kisling, J. W. (2006). Identity statuses and prosocial behaviors in young adulthood: A brief report. *Identity: An International Journal of Theory and Research, 6*(4), 363–69.

Hassrick, R. B. (1964). *The Sioux: Life and customs of a warrior society.* Norman, OK: University of Oklahoma Press.

Hastings, A. W. (2007). L. Frank Baum's editorials on the Sioux Nation. Retrieved from http://www.northern.edu/hastingw/baumedts.htm #sitting.

HeavyRunner, I., & DeCelles, R. (2002). Family education model: Meeting the student retention challenge. *Journal of American Indian Education, 41*(2), 29–37.

Herman-Stahl, M., Spencer, J., Aaroe, L. E., & Duncan, J. (2003). The implications of cultural orientation for substance use among American Indians. *American Indian and Alaska Native Mental Health Research, 11*(1), 46–66.

Hermes, M. (2007). Moving toward the language: Reflections on teaching in an Indigenous-immersion school. *Journal of American Indian Education, 46*(3), 54–71.

Hill, B., Vaughn, C., & Brooks Harrison, S. (1995). Living and working in two worlds: Case studies of five American Indian women teachers. *Clearing House, 69*(1), 42–49.

Hill, D. L. (2009). Relationship between sense of belonging as connectedness and suicide in American Indians. *Archives of Psychiatric Nursing, 23*(1), 63–74.

Hodson, J. (2004). Learning and healing: A wellness pedagogy for Aboriginal teacher education. Master's thesis, Brock University, St. Catharines, Ontario, Canada.

Hornberger, N. (2008). *Can schools save indigenous languages? Policy and practice on four continents.* Basingstoke, UK: Palgrave Macmillan.

Horse, P. G. (2005). Native American identity. *New Directions for Student Services, 109*(1), 61–68.

Huffman, T. (2001). Resistance theory and the transculturation hypothesis as explanations of college attrition and persistence among culturally traditional American Indian students. *Journal of American Indian Education, 40*(3), 1–23.

Huffman, T. (2003). A comparison of personal assessments of the college experience among reservation and nonreservation American Indian students. *Journal of American Indian Education, 42*(2), 1–16.

Huffman, T. (2008). *American Indian higher educational experiences: Cultural visions and personal journeys.* New York: Peter Lang.

Huffman, T. (2010). *Theoretical perspectives on American Indian education: Taking a new look at academic success and the achievement gap.* Lanham, MD: AltaMira Press.

Huffman, T. (2011). Plans to live on a reservation following college among American Indian students: An examination of transculturation theory. *Journal of Research in Rural Education, 26*(3), 1–13.

Huffman, T. (2013). *American Indian educators in reservation schools.* Reno, NV: University of Nevada Press.

Huffman, T., Sill, M., and Brokenleg, M. (1986). College achievement among Sioux and white South Dakota students. *Journal of American Indian Education, 25*(2), 32–38.

Ingalls, L., Hammond, H., Dupoux, E., & Baeza, R. (2006). Teachers' cultural knowledge and understanding of American Indian students and their families: Impact of culture on a child's learning. *Rural Special Education Quarterly, 25*(1), 16–24.

Inglebret, E., Jones, C., & CHiXapkaid (D. Michael Pavel). (2008). Integrating American Indian/Alaska Native culture into shared storybook intervention. *Language, Speech, and Hearing Services in Schools, 39,* 521–27.

Jackson, A. P., Smith, S. A., & Hill, C. L. (2003). Academic persistence among Native American college students. *Journal of College Student Development, 44*(4), 548–65.

James, K., Chavez, E., Beauvais, F., Edwards, R., & Oetting, G. (1995). School achievement and dropout among Anglo and Indian females and males: A comparative examination. *American Indian Culture and Research Journal, 19*(3), 181–206.

Jensen, E. (2009). *Teaching with poverty in mind: What being poor does to kids' brains and what schools can do about it.* Alexandria, VA: Association for Supervision and Curriculum Development.

Johnson, T., & Tomren, H. (1999). Helplessness, hopelessness, and despair: Identifying the precursors to Indian youth suicide. *American Indian Culture and Research Journal, 23*(3), 287–301.

Jones, M. G., Jones, B. D., & Hargrove, T. (2003). *The unintended consequences of high-stakes testing.* Lanham, MD: Rowman & Littlefield.

Josephy, A. (1974). *The Patriot chiefs: A chronicle of American Indian resistance.* New York: Viking Press.

Juneau, C. (2006). Building on yesterday, looking to tomorrow. *Phi Delta Kappan, 88*(3), 217.

Juntunen, C. L., Barraclough, D. J., Broneck, C. L., Seibel, G. A., Winrow, S. A., & Morin, P. M. (2001). American Indian perspectives on the career journey. *Journal of Counseling Psychology, 48*(3), 274–85.

Katz, M. (1986). *In the shadow of the poorhouse: A social history of welfare in America.* New York: Basic Books.

Katz, M. (1989). *The undeserving poor: From the war on poverty to the war on welfare.* New York: Pantheon.

Keith, A. L. (2004). *Sacred children, sacred teachers: Addressing the future of First Nations education.* Delta, BC: Healing the Land Publishing.

Kelting-Gibson, L. (2006). Preparing educators to meet the challenge of Indian Education for All. *Phi Delta Kappan, 88*(3), 204–7.

Kenyon, D. B., & Carter, J. S. (2011). Ethnic identity, sense of community, and psychological well-being among Northern Plains American Indian youth. *Journal of Community Psychology, 39*(1), 1–9.

Kitchen, J., Cherubini, L., Trudeau, L., & Hodson, J. (2009). Aboriginal education as cultural brokerage: New Aboriginal teachers reflect on language and culture in the classroom. *McGill Journal of Education, 44*(3), 355–75.

Klug, B., & Whitfield, P. (2003). *Widening the circle: Culturally relevant pedagogy for American Indian children.* New York: Routledge Falmer.

Kroger, J., Martinussen, M., & Marcia, J. E. (2010). Identity status change during adolescence and young adulthood: A meta-analysis. *Journal of Adolescence, 33*(5), 683–98.

Kulis, S., Napoli, M., & Marsiglia, F. (2002). The effects of ethnic pride and biculturalism on the drug use norms of urban American Indian adolescents in the Southwest. *Social Work Research, 26*(2), 101–12.

Ladson-Billings, G. (1999). Just what is critical race theory and what's it doing in a nice field like education? In L. Parker, D. Deyhle, & S. Villenas (Eds.), *Race is . . . race isn't: Critical race theory and qualitative studies in education* (pp. 7–30). Boulder, CO: Westview Press.

Lakota Dakota Nakota Language Preservation Summit (2014, October). *Prayer and Introductory Remarks.* 7th Annual Lakota Dakota Nakota Language Preservation Summit, Rapid City, South Dakota.

Laughter, J. C., Baker, A. A., Williams, S. M., Cearley, N. K., & Milner, H. R. (2006). The power of story: How personal narratives show us what teachers can do to fight racism. In E. W. Ross & V. O Pang (Eds.), *Race, ethnicity, and education,* Vol. 3, *Racial identity in education* (pp. 147–66). Westport, CT: Praeger Books.

Leavitt, R. (1995). Language and cultural content in Native education. In M. Battiste & J. Barman (Eds.), *First Nations education in Canada: The circle unfolds* (pp. 124–38). Vancouver, BC: University of British Columbia Press.

Ledlow, S. (1992). Is cultural discontinuity an adequate explanation for dropping out? *Journal of American Indian Education, 31*(3), 21–36.

Lee, M. B. (2013). *Success Academy: How Native American students prepare for college (and how colleges can prepare for them).* New York: Peter Lang.

Lee, T. S. (2009). Building Native nations through Native students' commitment to their communities. *Journal of American Indian Education, 48*(1), 19–36.

Lewis, O. (1959). *Five families: Mexican case studies in the culture of poverty.* New York: Basic Books.

Lindley, L. (2009). A tribal critical race theory analysis of academic achievement: A qualitative analysis of sixteen Arapaho women who earned degrees at the University of Wyoming. Doctoral dissertation, University of Wyoming, Laramie, WY.

Lipka, J., Sharp, N., Brenner, B., Yanez, E., & Sharp, F. (2005). The relevance of culturally based curriculum and instruction: The case of Nancy Sharp. *Journal of American Indian Education, 44*(3), 31–54.

Littlebear, R. (1999). Some rare and radical ideas for keeping Indigenous languages alive. In J. Reyhner, Cantoni, G., St. Clair, R. & Yazzie, E. P. (Eds.), *Revitalizing Indigenous languages* (pp. 1–5). Flagstaff, AZ: Northern Arizona University Press.

Little Soldier, L. (1997). Is there an "Indian" in your classroom? Working successfully with urban Native American students. *Phi Delta Kappan, 78*(8), 650–53.

Lloyd, D. O. (1961). Comparison of standardized test results of Indian and non-Indian in an integrated school system. *Journal of American Indian Education, 1*(1), 8–16.

Lomawaima, K. T. (1994). *They called it prairie light: The story of Chilocco Indian School.* Lincoln, NE: University of Nebraska Press.

Lomawaima, K. T. (1995). Educating Native Americans. In J. Banks & C. McGee (Eds.), *Handbook of research on multicultural education* (pp. 331–42). New York: Macmillan.

Lomawaima, K. T., & McCarty, T. (2006). *"To remain an Indian": Lessons in democracy from a century of Native American education.* New York: Teachers College Press.

Lovelace, S., & Wheeler, T. R. (2006). Cultural discontinuity between home and school language socialization patterns: Implications for teachers. *Education, 127*(2), 303–9.

Lysne, M., & Levy, G. D. (1997). Differences in ethnic identity in Native American adolescents as a function of school context. *Journal of Adolescent Research, 12*(3), 372–88.

Marcia, J. (1966). Development and validation of ego identity status. *Journal of Personality and Social Psychology, 3,* 551–58.

Marcia, J. (1980). Identity in adolescence. In J. Adelson (Ed.), *Handbook of adolescent psychology* (pp. 159–87). New York: Wiley.

Marcia, J., Waterman, A., Matteson, D., Archer, S., & Orlofsky, J. (1993). *Ego identity: A handbook for psychosocial research.* New York: Springer-Verlag.

Markstrom, C. A. (2010). Identity formation of American Indian adolescents: Local, national, and global considerations. *Journal of Research on Adolescence, 21*(2), 519–35.

Márquez Lavine, A. P. (2011). Parents' and teachers' views about heritage language at home and in school. Master's thesis, Eastern Washington University, Cheney, WA.

Marshall, J. M. (2004). *The journey of Crazy Horse: A Lakota history.* New York: Viking Press.

Marsiglia, F. F., Kulis, S., & Hecht, M. L. (2001). Ethnic labels and ethnic identity as predictors of drug use among middle school students in the Southwest. *Journal of Research on Adolescence, 11,* 21–48.

Martinez, D. (2014). School culture and American Indian educational outcomes. *Procedia—Social and Behavioral Sciences, 116,* 199–205.

Martin-McDonald, K., & McCarthy, A. (2008). "Marking" the white terrain in indigenous health research: Literature review. *Journal of Advanced Nursing, 61*(2), 126–33.

McCarty, T. (2002). *A place to be Navajo: Rough Rock and the struggle for self-determination in indigenous schooling.* Mahwah, NJ: Lawrence Erlbaum Associates.

McCarty, T. (2008). American Indian, Alaska Native, and Native Hawaiian education in the era of standardization and NCLB—An introduction. *Journal of American Indian Education, 47*(1), 1–9.

McCarty, T., Wallace, S., Lynch, R., & Benally, A. (1991). Classroom inquiry and Navajo learning styles: A call for reassessment. *Anthropology & Education Quarterly, 22*(1), 42–59.

McDonnell, L. M., & Weatherford, M. S. (2013). Organized interests and the Common Core. *Educational Researcher, 42*(9), 488–97.

McGillycuddy, V. T. (1929). "Narrative of the life of Crazy Horse." *Nebraska History Magazine, 19,* 36–38.

McIntosh, P. (2006). White Privilege: Unpacking the invisible knapsack. In E. Lee, D. Menkart, & M. Okazawa-Rey (Eds.), *Beyond heroes and holidays* (pp. 83–86). Washington, DC: Teaching for Change.

Mihesuah, D. A. (2003). Basic empowering strategies for the classroom. *American Indian Quarterly, 27*(1/2), 459–78.

Miller, F. (1971). Involvement in an urban university. In J. Waddell (Ed.), *The American Indian in urban society* (pp. 312–40). Boston, MA: Little, Brown.

Moeller, M., Anderson, C., & Grosz, L. (2012). Six elements of diversity: Teacher candidate perceptions after engaging Native American students. *Journal of Invitational Theory and Practice, 18*(1), 3–10.

Mohatt, G. V., Trimble, J., & Dickson, R. A. (2006). Psychosocial foundations of academic performance in culture-based education programs for American Indian and Alaska Native youth: Reflections on a multidisciplinary perspective. *Journal of American Indian Education, 45*(3), 38–59.

Morgan, H. (2009). What every teacher needs to know to teach Native American students. *Multicultural Education, 16*(4), 10–12.

Morris, R., Pae, H. K., Arrington, C., & Sevick, R. (2006). The assessment challenge of Native American educational researchers. *Journal of American Indian Education, 45*(3), 77–91.

Murguiá, E., Padilla, R., & Pavel, M. (1991). Ethnicity and the concept of social integration in Tinto's model of institutional departure. *Journal of College Student Development, 32,* 433–39.

Myer, D. S. (1970). *An autobiography of Dillon S. Myer/1970*. Bancroft Library, University of California, Berkeley, Oral History Transcript.

Myer, D. S. (1971). *Uprooted Americans: The Japanese Americans and the War Relocation Authority during World War II*. Tucson, AZ: University of Arizona Press.

Nagel, J. (1996). *American Indian ethnic renewal: Red power and the resurgence of identity and culture*. New York: Oxford University Press.

Nam, Y., Roehrig, G., Kern, A., & Reynolds, B. (2012). Perceptions and practices of culturally relevant science teaching in American Indian classrooms. *International Journal of Science and Mathematics Education, 11*, 143–67.

Neuman, S. B. (2008). *Educating the other America: Top experts tackle poverty, literacy, and achievement in our schools*. Baltimore, MD: Paul H. Brookes.

Ng, J., & Rury, J. (2005). Poverty and education: A critical analysis of the Ruby Payne phenomenon. *Teachers College Record, 105*(3), 490–519.

Ngai, P. B. (2008). An emerging Native language education framework for reservation public schools with mixed populations. *Journal of American Indian Education, 47*(2), 22–50.

Ogbu, J. (1978). *Minority education and caste: The American system in cross-cultural perspective*. New York: Academic Press.

Ogbu, J. (1981). School ethnography: A multilevel approach. *Anthropology & Education Quarterly, 13*(4), 3–29.

Ogbu, J. (1982). Cultural discontinuities and schooling. *Anthropology & Education Quarterly, 13*(4), 290–307.

Ogbu, J. (1987). Variability in minority school performance: A problem in search of an explanation. *Anthropology & Education Quarterly, 18*(4), 312–34.

Ogbu, J. (1991). Minority coping responses and school experiences. *Journal of Psychohistory, 18*(4), 433–56.

Ogbu, J. (1992). Adaptation to minority status and impact on school success. *Theory into Practice, 31*(4), 287–95.

Ogbu, J. (2003). *Black American students in an affluent suburb: A study of academic disengagement*. Mahwah, NJ: Lawrence Erlbaum Associates.

Ogbu, J., & Simons, H. (1998). Voluntary and involuntary minorities: A cultural-ecological theory of school performance with some implications for education. *Anthropology & Education Quarterly, 29*(2), 155–88.

Okagaki, L., Helling, M. K., & Bingham, G. E. (2009). American Indian college students' ethnic identity and beliefs about education. *Journal of College Student Development, 50*(2), 157–76.

Osei-Kofi, N. (2005). Pathologizing the poor: A framework for understanding Ruby Payne's work. *Equity & Excellence in Education, 38*(4), 367–75.

Pavel, M., Banks, S. R., & Pavel, S. (2002). The Osale story: Training teachers for schools serving American Indians and Alaska Natives. *Journal of American Indian Education, 41*(2), 38–47.

Payne, R. (2005). *A framework for understanding poverty* (4th ed.). Highlands, TX: Aha! Process.

Peshkin, A. (1997). *Places of memory: Whiteman's schools and Native American communities.* New York: Routledge.

Pewewardy, C. (1998a). Our children can't wait: Recapturing the essence of Indigenous schools in the United States. *Cultural Survival Quarterly, 22*(1), 22–34.

Pewewardy, C. (1998b). Fluff and feathers: Treatment of American Indians in the literature and the classroom. *Equity Excellence Education, 31*(1), 69–76.

Pewewardy, C. (1999). The holistic medicine wheel: An Indigenous model of teaching and learning. *Winds of Change, 14*(1), 28–31.

Pewewardy, C. (2002). Learning styles of American Indian / Alaska Native students: A review of the literature and implications for practice. *Journal of American Indian Education, 41*(3), 22–56.

Pewewardy, C., & Fitzpatrick, M. (2009). Working with American Indian students and families. *Intervention in School and Clinic, 45*(2), 91–98.

Philips, S. (1983). *The invisible culture: Communication and community on the Warm Springs reservation.* New York: Longman.

Phillips, J. (2014). A changing epidemiology of suicide? The influence of birth cohorts on suicide rates in the United States. *Social Science and Medicine, 114,* 151–60.

Phinney, J. (1989). Stages of ethnic identity in minority group adolescents. *Journal of Early Adolescence, 9*(1–2), 34–49.

Phinney, J. (1990). Ethnic identification in adolescents and adults: Review of research. *Psychological Bulletin, 108*(3), 499–514.

Phinney, J. (2000). Identity formation across cultures: The interaction of personal, societal, and historical change. *Human Development, 43*(1), 27–31.

Pidgeon, M. (2008). Pushing against the margins: Indigenous theorizing of "success" and retention in higher education. *Journal of College Student Retention, 10*(3), 339–60.

Powers, K. M. (2005). Promoting school achievement among American Indian students throughout the school years. *Childhood Education, 81*(6), 338–42.

Powers, K. M. (2006). An exploratory study of cultural identity and culture-based educational programs for urban American Indian students. *Urban Education, 41*(1), 20–49.

Powers, K., Potthoff, S. J., Bearinger, L. H., & Resnick, M. D. (2003). Does cultural programming improve educational outcomes for American Indian youth? *Journal of American Indian Education, 42*(2), 17–49.

Powers, T. (2010). *The killing of Crazy Horse.* New York: Vintage Books.

Pratt, R. (1973). The advantages of mingling Indians with whites. In Francis Paul Prucha (Ed.), *Americanizing the American Indians: Writings by the "Friends of the Indian," 1880–1900* (pp. 260–71). Cambridge, MA: Harvard University Press.

Rains, F. (2002). From the eyes of the colonized: Rethinking the legacy of colonization and its impact on American Indians. *Journal of Philosophy and History of Education, 52,* 161–70.

Rains, F. (2003). To greet the dawn with open eyes: American Indians, white privilege, and the power of residual guilt in the social studies. In G. Ladson-Billings (Ed.), *Critical race theory perspectives on social studies: The profession, policies, and curriculum* (pp. 199–230). Greenwich, CT: Information Age Publishing.

Ravitch, D. (2010). *The death and life of the great American school system: How testing and choice are undermining education.* New York: Basic Books.

Rendon, L., Jalomo, R., & Nora, A. (2002). Theoretical considerations in the study of minority student retention in higher education. In J. M. Braxton (Ed.), *Reworking the student departure puzzle* (pp. 127–56). Nashville, TN: Vanderbilt University Press.

Reyhner, J. (1992). American Indians out of school: A review of school-based causes and solutions. *Journal of American Indian Education, 31*(2), 37–56.

Reyhner, J., & Eder, J. (2004). *American Indian education: A history.* Norman, OK: University of Oklahoma Press.

Robinson-Zanartu, C., & Majel-Dixon, J. (1996). Parental voices: American Indian relationships with schools. *Journal of American Indian Education, 36*(1), 33–54.

Roithmayr, D. (1999). Introduction to critical race theory in educational research and praxis. In L. Parker, D. Deyhle, & S. Villenas (Eds.), *Race is . . . race isn't: Critical race theory and qualitative studies in education* (pp. 1–6). Boulder, CO: Westview Press.

Romero-Little, M. E. (2010). How should young Indigenous children be prepared for learning? A vision of early childhood education for Indigenous children. *Journal of American Indian Education, 49*(1/2), 7–27.

Rosier, P. (2009). *Serving their country: American Indian politics and patriotism in the twentieth century.* Cambridge, MA: Harvard University Press.

Rothenberg, P. S. (2005). *White privilege.* New York: Worth Publishers.

Rowley, S. J., Sellers, R. M., Chavous, T. M., & Smith, M. A. (1998). The relationship between racial identity and self-esteem in African American college and high school students. *Journal of Personality and Social Psychology, 74,* 715–24.

Ruff, W. G. (2014). Identity, heritage and achievement: A comparative case study of effective education in Indian country. *Researcher, 26*(1), 18–22.

Ryan, W. (1976). *Blaming the victim.* New York: Vintage Press.

Sanders, D. (1987). Cultural conflicts: An important factor in the academic failure of American Indian students. *Journal of Multicultural Counseling and Development, 15*(1), 81–90.

Sandoz, M. (1942). *Crazy Horse, the strange man of the Oglalas: A biography.* New York: Hastings House.

Scott, W. J. (1986). Attachment to Indian culture and the "difficult situation": A study of American Indian college students. *Youth and Society, 17*(4), 381–95.

Senese, G. (1991). *Self-determination and the social education of Native Americans.* New York: Praeger.

Smith, P. C., & Warrior, R. A. (1996). *Like a hurricane: The Indian movement from Alcatraz to Wounded Knee.* New York: Free Press.

Smith-Mohamed, K. (1998). Role models, mentors, and Native students: Some implications for educators. *Canadian Journal of Native Education, 22*(2), 238–59.

Solorzano, D., & Yosso, T. (2002). Critical race methodology: Counter-story-telling as an analytical framework for education research. *Qualitative Inquiry, 8*(1), 23–44.

Sparks, S. (2000). Classroom and curriculum accommodations for Native American students. *Intervention in School and Clinic, 35,* 259–63.

Stairs, A. (1995). Learning processes and teaching roles in Native education: Cultural base and cultural brokerage. In M. Battiste & J. Barman (Eds.), *First Nations education in Canada: The circle unfolds* (pp. 139–53). Vancouver, BC: University of British Columbia Press.

St. Germaine, R. (1995). *Drop-out rates among American Indian and Alaska Native students: Beyond cultural discontinuity.* Retrieved from https://eric.ed.gov/?q=ED388492.

Stiffman, R. A., Brown, E., Freedenthal, S., House, L., Ostmann, E., & Yu, M. S. (2007). American Indian youth: Personal, familial, and environmental strengths. *Journal of Child and Family Studies, 16,* 331–46.

Strong, W. C. (1998, April). Low expectations by teachers within an academic context. *Paper presented at the annual meeting of the American Educational Research Association.* San Diego, CA.

Swaney, E. (2006). The challenge of IEFA. *Phi Delta Kappan, 88*(3), 190–91.

Swisher, K., & Tippeconnic, J. (Eds.). (1999). *Next steps: Research and practice to advance Indian education.* Charleston, WV: Clearinghouse on Rural Education and Small Schools.

Szasz, M. C. (1999). *Education and the American Indian: The road to self-determination since 1928.* Albuquerque, NM: University of New Mexico Press.

Tajfel, H. (1978). *The social psychology of minorities.* New York, NY: Minority Rights Group.

Tajfel, H. (1981). *Human groups and social categories.* Cambridge, UK: Cambridge University Press.

Tall Bull, L. (2006). Preserving our histories for those yet to be born. *Phi Delta Kappan, 88*(3), 192.

Taylor, F. L. (2005). American Indian women in higher education: Is Tinto's model applicable? Master's thesis, Montana State University, Bozeman, MT.

Tharp, R. G. (2006). Four hundred years of evidence: Culture, pedagogy, and Native America. *Journal of American Indian Education, 45*(2), 6–25.

Thornton, R. (1987). *American Indian holocaust and survival: A population history since 1492.* Norman, OK: University of Oklahoma Press.

Tierney, W. G. (1992). An anthropological analysis of student participation in college. *Journal of Higher Education, 63*(6), 603–18.

Tinto, V. (1987). *Leaving college: Rethinking the causes and cures of student attrition,* 1st ed. Chicago: University of Chicago Press.

Tinto, V. (1988). Stages of student departure: Reflections on the longitudinal character of student leaving. *Journal of Higher Education, 59*(4), 438–55.

Tippeconnic, J. W., & Tippeconnic Fox, M. J. (2012). American Indian tribal values: A critical consideration in the education of American Indian / Alaska Natives today. *International Journal of Qualitative Studies in Education, 25*(7), 841–53.

Toomey, R. B., & Umaña-Taylor, A. J. (2012). The role of ethnic identity on self-esteem for ethnic minority youth. *Prevention Researcher, 19*(2), 8–12.

Trafzer, C. E., Keller, J. A., & Sisquoc, L. (2006). Introduction: Origin and development of the American Indian boarding school system. In C. E. Trafzer, J. A. Keller, & L. Sisquoc (Eds.), *Boarding school blues: Revisiting American Indian educational experiences* (pp. 1–34). Lincoln, NE: University of Nebraska Press.

Ulrich, R. (2010). *American Indian nations from termination to restoration, 1953–2006.* Lincoln, NE: University of Nebraska Press.

Umaña-Taylor, A. J. (2011). Ethnic identity. In S. J. Schwartz, K. Luyckx, & V. Vignoles (Eds.), *Handbook of identity theory and research* (pp. 791–809). New York: Springer.

US Census Bureau. (2010). *The American Indian and Alaska Native population, 2010.* Washington, DC: US Printing Office.

Valdas, R. E. (1995). Assessing the relationship between academic performance and attachment to Navajo. *Journal of Navajo Education, 12*(2), 16–25.

Valencia, R. R. (2010). *Dismantling contemporary deficit thinking: Educational thought and practice.* New York: Routledge.

Vanderwerth, W. C. (1971). *Indian oratory: Famous speeches by noted Indian chieftains.* Norman, OK: University of Oklahoma Press.

Van Hamme, L. (1996). American Indian cultures and the classroom. *Journal of American Indian Education, 35*(2), 21–34.

Vaught, S., & Castagno, A. (2008). "I don't think I'm a racist": Critical race theory, teacher attitudes, and structural racism. *Race, Ethnicity and Education, 11*(2), 95–113.

Vestal, S. (1934). *New sources of Indian history, 1850–1891: The Ghost Dance, the prairie Sioux—a miscellany.* Norman, OK: University of Oklahoma Press.

Ward, C. J. (2005). *Native Americans in the school system: Family, community, and academic achievement.* Lanham, MD: AltaMira Press.

Ward, M. K. (2011). Teaching indigenous American culture and history: Perpetuating knowledge or furthering intellectual colonization? *Journal of Social Sciences, 7*(2), 104–12.

Warren, W. Z. (2006). One teacher's story: Creating a new future or living up to our own history? *Phi Delta Kappan, 88*(3), 198–203.

Wax, R. H. (1967). *The warrior dropouts.* Lawrence, KS: University Press of Kansas.

Waxman, S. (2003, January). Abuse charges hit reservation church-run schools cited in wide-ranging lawsuit. *Washington Post*, p. A01.

Werito, V. (2013). Diné youth and identity in education. In J. Reyhner, J. Martin, L. Lockard, & W. S. Gilbert (Eds.), *Honoring our children: Culturally appropriate approaches for teaching Indigenous students.* Flagstaff, AZ: Northern Arizona University Press.

Weyler, R. (1992). Blood of the land: The government and corporate war against First Nations. Philadelphia, PA: New Society Publishers.

Whitbeck, L., Hoyt, D., Stubben, J., & LaFromboise, T. (2001). Traditional culture and academic success among American Indian children in the upper Midwest. *Journal of American Indian Education, 40*(2), 48–60.

White Shield, R. (2009). Identifying and understanding Indigenous cultural spiritual strengths in the higher education experience of Indigenous women. *Wicaza Sa Review, 24*(1), 47–63.

Wilkinson, C. (2005). *Blood struggle: The rise of modern Indian nations.* New York: Norton.

Wilson, A. C. (2004). Reclaiming our humanity: Decolonization and the recovery of Indigenous knowledge. In D. A. Milhesuah & A. C. Wilson (Eds.), *Indigenizing the academy* (pp. 69–87). Lincoln, NE: University of Nebraska Press.

Winstead, T., Lawrence, A., Brantmeier, E., & Frey, C. (2008). Language, sovereignty, cultural contestation, and American Indian schools: No Child Left Behind and a Navajo test case. *Journal of American Indian Education, 47*(1), 46–64.

Wood, P., & Clay, W. C. (1996). Perceived structural barriers and academic performance among American Indian high school students. *Youth and Society, 28*(1), 40–61.

Woodard, S. (2011, August 9). Native American sex-abuse lawsuits head for a higher court. [Blog post] Retrieved from http://www.huffingtonpost.com/stephanie-woodard/south-dakota-sex-abuse-pl_b_851837.html.

Woodrum, A. (2009). Cultural identity and schooling in rural New Mexico. *Journal of Research in Rural Education, 24*(8), 1–5.

Writer, J. H., & Oesterreich, H. A. (2011). Native women teacher candidates "with strength": Rejecting deficits and restructuring institutions. *Action in Teacher Education, 33*(5/6), 509–23.

Yazzie, T. (1999). Culturally appropriate curriculum: A research-based rationale. In K. C. Swisher & J. W. Tippeconnic (Eds.), *Next steps: Research and practice to advance Indian education* (pp. 83–106). Charleston, WV: Clearinghouse on Rural Education and Small Schools.

Yazzie-Mintz, T. (2007). From a place deep inside: Culturally appropriate curriculum as the embodiment of Navajo-ness in classroom pedagogy. *Journal of American Indian Education, 46*(3), 72–93.

Yin, R. K. (2014). *Case study research: Designs and methods* (5th ed.). Thousand Oaks, CA: Sage.

Yosso, T. J. (2005). Whose culture has capital? A critical race theory discussion of community cultural wealth. *Race, Ethnicity and Education, 8*(1), 69–91.

Zahrt, E. G. (2001). Do reservation Native Americans vote with their feet? A re-examination of Native American migration, 1985–1990. *American Journal of Economics and Sociology, 60*(4), 815–27.

# Index

Rowley, S. J., 71
Ruff, W. G., 49, 122
Rury, J., 15
Ryan, W., 14

San Carlos Apache tribe, 1, 3
Sanders, D., 111
Sandoz, M., 138
Scott, W. J., 15, 18, 19, 73
Seidman, E., 71
self-determination, 11–13
Sellers, R. M., 71
Semingson, P., 15
Senese, G., 113
Sevick, R., 140
Sherman Indian High School, 138
Sill, M., 73
Simons, H., 113
Simpson, G., 138
*Sioux: Life and Customs of a Warrior Society, The,* 139
Sisquoc, L., 6
Sitting Bull, 21–25, 30, 32, 118, 136
Sharp, F., 91
Sharp, N., 91
Sheridan, Philip, 133
Smith, M. A., 71
Smith, P. C., 11, 135
Smith, S. A., 111
Smith-Mohamed, K., 56
Smythe, H., 14
Solorzano, D., 114
South Dakota State University, 75, 76
Sparks, S., 91
Spaulding, J. A., 138
Spencer, J., 72
Spotted Tail Agency, 138
Stairs, Arlene, 50
Standing Rock reservation, North Dakota, 22, 136
Stefancic, J., 114, 115, 142
stereotypes of American Indian students, 87, 88, 96
St. Francis Indian School, 12
St. Germaine, R., 113
Stiffman, R. A., 71
St. Joseph Indian School, 12
Strong, W. C., 96
structural inequality theory, 109, 112–14, 141
Stubben, J., 19
Success Academy, 75, 76

Swaney, Ellen, 95
Swisher, K., 16, 54, 89, 91
Sypolt, Diane Gilbert, 133, 134
Szasz, M., 5

Tajfel, H., 71
Tall Bull, Lynwood, 123
Taylor, F. L., 141
*Teaching with Poverty in Mind,* 101
Terhune, M. N., 49
termination, 7–11, 13, 134, 135
Termination Act, 8
Tharp, Roland, 19, 20, 89
*Theoretical Perspectives on American Indian Education,* 141
Thomas, K., 114
Thornton, Russell, 23
Tierney, W. G., 141
Tinto, Vincent, 141
Tippeconnic, J. W., 16, 54, 89–91
Tippeconnic Fox, M. J., 90
Tomren, H., 73
Toomey, R. B., 71
Torres-Rivera, E., 120
Tosawi (Silver Knife), 133
Trafzer, C. E., 6
Trail of Broken Treaties, 10, 135
transculturation theory, 109, 116–19, 141
tribal critical race theory, 115, 116, 142
tribal cultural preservation and schools, 108, 123, 124, 128, 130
tribal identity, 2, 4, 6, 18–20, 26, 29, 45, 52, 57, 65, 69, 70, 72–74, 85, 116, 118–20, 137; defined, 26; Native students' ambiguity and, 73, 76, 77, 82; Native students and, 53, 54, 62, 63, 68, 71, 73–79, 84, 99, 124, 117, 121, 126, 128; rival identities and, 80, 81
tribal legacy, 2, 19, 25, 26, 39, 44, 57, 63, 65, 78, 83, 98, 100, 102, 119, 126; defined, 25
tribal spirituality, 38, 57, 61, 72, 79, 82, 93, 94, 103, 104, 117, 127–30, 140, 141
tribal strengths, 2, 20, 21, 25–30, 45, 49, 52, 61, 63, 69, 70, 82, 83, 97, 103, 108, 116–19, 124, 125, 127, 129; defined, 25; educational success of Native students and, 21, 69, 73–76, 83, 120, 121, 124; professional efficacy of Native educators and, 55, 57, 60, 62; teaching Native students and, 45, 46, 58, 64, 98. *See also* tribal identity; tribal legacy